CUSTOM-MAKE
YOUR OWN
SHOES
AND HANDBAGS

CUSTOM-MAKE YOUR OWN SHOES AND HANDBAGS

A Simplified Method of Making Women's Shoes and Handbags at Home

by

Mary Wales Loomis

CROWN PUBLISHERS, INC., NEW YORK

To Richard,
who grew up thinking
all mothers made their own shoes

Library of Congress Cataloging in Publication Data

Loomis, Mary Wales.
  Custom-make your own shoes and handbags.

  Includes index.
  1. Boots and shoes. 2. Handbags. I. Title.
TT678.5.L66   646.4'8   77-13699
ISBN 0-517-53138-0
ISBN 0-517-53139-9

CONTENTS

ACKNOWLEDGMENTS

I wish to thank all the people through the years who have encouraged me in my pursuit of information about making shoes, including the shoe repairmen, leather company salesmen, and shoe store managers, all of whom have answered questions for me. I would also like to thank the people who discouraged me because it made me more determined to succeed.

Thanks to my husband, Robert Loomis, who has done such a wonderful job in illustrating and photographing. Thanks also to Robert for his help in writing and organizing the book.

My special thanks go to Louise Boggess, without whose literary assistance this book may not have been written.

PREFACE

Many women dream of owning a closetful of custom-made shoes. To many, it remains a dream. But you can make this dream come true if you learn to make your own shoes.

I have always designed and sewed my own clothes, including hats and bags. Many times, after designing an outfit, I wished for shoes to match. I determined to learn to make my own shoes.

To satisfy my curiosity about shoe construction, I began by tearing some sandals and bedroom slippers apart. Copying them appeared a simple project. Using the parts of the old shoes for the pattern, I made some velveteen sandals and gave them an added touch by embroidering the tops.

After making flat house-type slippers and sandals for a while, I couldn't resist the challenge of making a pair of pumps with heels. I kept experimenting until I developed a successful method. To further test the method, I taught some of my friends.

They in turn told their friends about me. After several local newspapers wrote feature articles about my unique project, strangers besieged me to teach them to make shoes. Recognition of my special and simple method for custom-making shoes increased with appearances on television and radio. The enthusiastic response from women showed me the need for a book on the subject.

Each woman differs greatly as to the reasons for wanting to make her own shoes. Finding solutions to these problems enabled me to expand information to answer any question. Instead of sacrificing comfort for style or style for comfort, you can actually custom-make your own shoes by following the instructions in this book.

I have taught private classes and now have joined the teaching staff of the College of San Mateo. These experiences assisted me in choosing the best way to project the information in this book.

Mary Wales Loomis
College of San Mateo
San Mateo, California

I
SHOES,
SHOES, SHOES
or How I Began to Make My Own Shoes

My doorbell rang urgently one evening around dinnertime. A strange woman pointed to the newspaper in one hand. "Forgive me for imposing on you this way, but I read about you in this paper. I'm in a hurry to catch a plane; but before I leave town, I've got to see your shoes."

I reluctantly led her to my bedroom. I opened the closet door revealing rows of see-through boxes on the shelf, each showing a pair of colorful shoes I had made. The woman squealed with delight as she inspected one pair after another. When she discovered we wore the same size, she tried on a pair. Then she posed and strutted around the bedroom saying, "Amazing! absolutely amazing!" In spite of the intrusion I felt complimented.

This marked the beginning of newspaper feature articles, along with television and radio appearances. A parade of women knocked on my door. Each wanted to learn how to make their own shoes.

One woman drove almost a hundred miles in a station wagon full of prospective shoemakers to see my creations. Whenever we go to a party, women want to try on my shoes, regardless of the size. The men usually show more curiosity about the details of construction.

Someone always asks, "*Why* did you want to make your own shoes?"

As the youngest of five girls, inevitably, I inherited their hand-me-down clothes. I ripped them apart and restyled them to retain my individuality. I didn't want my work to look "homemade" so I endeavored to make them look professional. When I decided to make shoes, I used some hat-making techniques in the process.

First I tore an old pair of shoes apart to study the construction. While I could duplicate the tops easily, the soles presented a problem. I couldn't use the old soles on a new pair of shoes! Needing advice, I went to see our neighborhood shoe repairman, Mario. Mario learned shoemaking in Italy long before he came to America. When I explained that I wanted to develop a "home sewing" method for making shoes with my regular sewing machine, he encouraged me enthusiastically.

"Use a pliable leather for the soles. You can cut and handle it easily," he advised. "Stiff leather would require special machinery, much too difficult for ladies!"

"But will it wear? Don't I need stiff leather for the soles?" I half argued.

He dismissed the questions with a wave of his hand. "Tooling leather will wear well enough for ladies' shoes."

"How do I fasten the soles to the bottom of the shoes?" I could see myself nailing and stitching them together, a tedious task.

He shrugged impatiently. "Shoemakers' cement—stronger than nails."

He told me where I could buy it. With this information I began the most interesting and money-saving project of my life.

At the Shoe Findings Company in San Francisco I inquired about supplies. When I explained my purpose, unlike Mario, they burst out laughing.

"Whoever heard of a lady making her own shoes; forget it," they advised.

I could see that they would never understand, but I insisted that they sell me the items I came to buy. Reluctantly, one man sold me the tooling leather and shoemakers' cement.

"You'll set shoemaking back a hundred years," he said, sadly shaking his head.

I rushed home and went to work on my first pair of shoes, a flat heeled T-strap sandal in bright red velveteen. For the tops of the shoes I used fabric on the outside, with buckram and felt for the shaping and stiffening, as I did with hats. That wonderful cement held the heel and sole securely. "Right, Mario, the sole poses no problem using pliable leather."

That Christmas my friends received slippers decorated with rhinestones, pearls, and mink on velvet and satin. One of my friends commented, "One of these days Mary'll probably try to make her own high heeled shoes."

My subconscious began working on this idea before I finished the sandals. When I made hats, I molded them over a block. In ceramics, I used to cast little figurines in plaster of Paris. Why not make such a mold to shape the shoe? By combining the two techniques I realized that I could fill a pair of my own good-fitting pumps with plaster of Paris and make a perfect cast of the inside of my shoes. I went to work immediately. When the plaster dried, I ripped the shoes apart and took all the pieces to show Mario. He explained about the different parts and their functions. The casts he called, in shoe language, *lasts*.

He referred to the top of the shoe as the *upper*. He picked up the cardboard composition shape that surrounds the heel. "A *counter*," he said. "This metal piece in the arch of the shoe we call a *shank*, and it keeps the arch of the shoe from collapsing."

When I took the coverings off the heels, I found them made of wood, but Mario said they use plastic for heels too. Most people know the little leather piece on the bottom of the heel as a *lift*.

Later at home I spread out all the pieces of the shoes on my worktable. Most of them I could make or salvage from old shoes, but I would need to buy some parts. What a relief to know I wouldn't need to nail anything as I could sew and cement the entire shoes.

For the first basic pump pattern I copied the horseshoe shape of the *upper* and added a small seam allowance. For the outside fabric of the upper, I chose wool plaid scraps from a skirt I made and sandwiched buckram inside before lining it with felt. After sewing these pieces together on my sewing machine I wet and formed these uppers over the plaster *lasts*. When I laced them across the bottoms with nylon yarn like a Thanksgiving turkey, I made the task more difficult because of the narrow allowance on my first pattern. While it didn't ruin the shoes, I immediately adjusted the pattern for the next pair.

By drying the uppers thoroughly before removing them from the *lasts*, the buckram will return to its original stiffness. I didn't want to sit around waiting for them to dry naturally, so I popped them into the oven with low heat to hasten the process. My husband came sniffing into the kitchen. "What's for dinner?" he asked.

"Shoes!"

He didn't believe me until he peeked into the oven.

To remove the uppers from the lasts I snipped away the nylon yarn stitching and slipped the lasts out of the open bottoms. From then on I predicted success since cementing the sole and heel would produce a pair of shoes.

When I finished that first pair of shoes, I put them on and danced all around the house shouting, "I can make my own shoes!"

Since that first attempt, I have made dozens of shoes: sandals, boots, pumps, all to match dresses, skirts, pants, or sometimes a handbag. Such matching catches the feminine eye, and women stop me in the supermarket or wherever with, "Pardon me, but I noticed your shoes."

I explain to them I make my own "from scratch," and they occasionally look at me in disbelief.

I have constantly improved my techniques, but my orginal concept proved a good one. I have not purchased shoes since I made the first pair.

When I went on vacation "back East," a friend who owns a shoe store in my hometown thoughtfully arranged for me to tour a shoe factory. For the first time I observed shoes made commercially. Naturally, I compared their method to mine. While I followed the same basic principle their procedure proved more complicated. The assembly line process dictates many steps that I have found unnecessary with my simplified method. As a result any home sewer with a standard sewing machine and strong motivation can make her own shoes. If you will work along with me, you can learn this easy method, which begins with making a last.

II
MAKING
YOUR LASTS

The lasts shape the shoes; consequently, your success with custom-made shoes depends on how well you form the lasts. Naturally, you must make a right and a left last that you can individually adjust to fit each foot.

You may choose one of two ways of making lasts. First, let's consider the simple way, using a pair of shoes.

THE SIMPLE METHOD
To make your master pattern and lasts, choose a pair of shoes that fits well. Think of this as a model of the shape of your foot, and the parts as master patterns for soles, innersoles, and uppers.

For your lasts choose a pair of pumps with closed heel and toe to contain the plaster. Naturally, the newer the shoes the smoother the lasts. If you select your old garden shoes for your lasts, your new shoes will duplicate the shape of those old shoes, lumps and all. In case you don't have a good pair of shoes to use for the lasts, try shopping at a shoe outlet or even a rummage sale for a bargain.

I know some people will quickly argue, "Never in my life have I bought a pair of shoes that fits comfortably; so how can I make lasts?" Right now I suggest that you go along with me and make a pair of lasts from any of your shoes, whether they fit exactly or not, to get the experience in making the patterns. You will become familiar with the parts of the shoe and how they should look. Better still, you can adjust the lasts for a custom fit.

Select your time for this project. Take the phone off the hook and put the animals out. Of course, you don't want the children around either to distract you.

1. Materials Needed

Collect the materials before you start:

Newspapers to spread on the floor and use in cleaning up plaster of Paris.

Two plastic bowls, 2 quart capacity: one for mixing plaster and one for washing your hands.

Ten pounds of casting plaster of Paris. Buy this at a hardware or paint store.

Large metal spoon for mixing the plaster.

⅛ cup cooking oil or Vaseline to oil the inside of the shoes before you fill them with plaster.

Utility knife for cutting the upper away from the sole when the plaster dries.

Medium size screwdriver, hammer, and standard size pliers for taking the shoes apart.

Several large pieces of lightweight cardboard or heavy paper for making patterns.

Fairly heavy cardboard, "gift box" weight to attach to the bottoms of the lasts.   *shoes , nylons*

Spread the newspapers over an area of 5 square feet because this process makes a mess. Before you begin to work with the plaster of Paris, please read the instructions on the label. If you let any plaster get into your sink or drain, it will clog the plumbing. Keep one of the bowls filled with warm water to wash your hands occasionally so you won't forget and rinse them in the sink.

2. Preparing the Shoes

Remove any trimming from the shoes, such as buckles or bows. Save them as you may want to copy or use them for a trim on the shoes you make. Put the insoles aside for a pattern.

Make a slit in the tops of the shoes near the toes for air to escape. If you don't do this, the plaster may trap an air bubble in the toe of the shoe and leave a hole in the last (see Figure 1).

Thoroughly grease the inside of the shoes with oil or Vaseline. Spread the oil all around inside the shoe with your fingers as shown in Figures 2a and b. I didn't oil the inside of the first pair of shoes I filled with plaster, and I almost didn't get the forms out of the shoes. By the time I did cast good lasts, I used all the shoes in my closet plus a couple of pairs belonging to a friend who wore the same size.

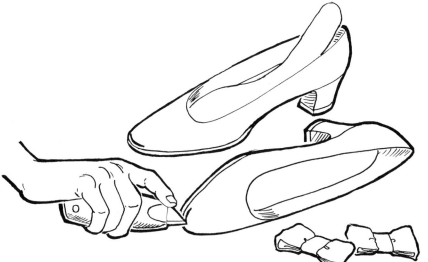

Fig. 1.
Slit the tops of the shoes for an air escape.

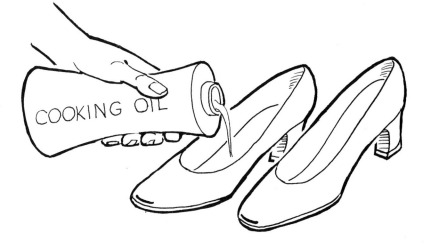

Fig. 2a.
Oil the insides of the shoes.

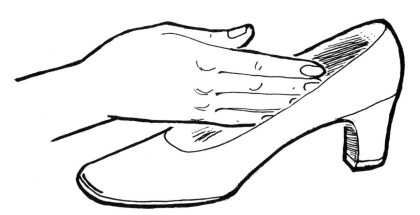

Fig. 2b.
Spread the oil all around the inside of the shoes with your fingers.

Put two cups of cool water into one of the bowls. Fill the other with warm water to use for washing your hands. *Never use the sink.* Plaster dries the skin, so keep a bottle of hand lotion nearby. This amount of plaster should fill one shoe of average size. Do only one shoe at a time.

Slowly spoon four (4) cups of plaster of Paris into the two (2) cups of cool water. Stir until the mixture looks smooth and creamy. It will be the consistency of heavy cake batter. When the mixture goes "glop, glop" as you stir it, use immediately. If you continue stirring after this consistency, you hasten the hardening of the plaster.

Spoon the plaster into the toe of the shoe. Tap on the sole of the shoe with the spoon to bring air bubbles to the surface. Continue spooning the plaster into the shoe until you fill it, building the top of the instep to a slight bulge. Dip your hands into the washing bowl frequently and smooth the top of the plaster. Keep your hand wet while you build a shape that looks very much like the foot itself in the shoe. Set the plaster-filled shoe aside to harden. Follow the illustrations in Figures 3a, b, c, d, e, and f.

Fig. 3a.
Add the plaster of Paris to the cool water.

Fig. 3b.
Stir the plaster of Paris into the water until it looks smooth and creamy.

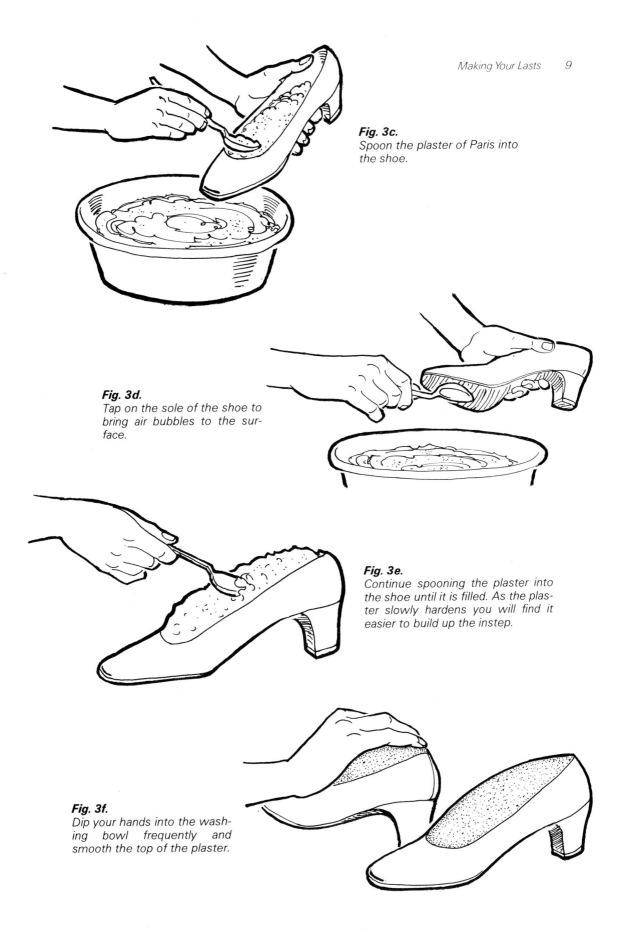

Fig. 3c.
Spoon the plaster of Paris into the shoe.

Fig. 3d.
Tap on the sole of the shoe to bring air bubbles to the surface.

Fig. 3e.
Continue spooning the plaster into the shoe until it is filled. As the plaster slowly hardens you will find it easier to build up the instep.

Fig. 3f.
Dip your hands into the washing bowl frequently and smooth the top of the plaster.

If you have some plaster left over, scrape it out and clean the bowl with wet newspapers, then with paper towels. Do not mix any leftover plaster with the new batch, or you will get lumps.

Fill the other shoe according to the same procedure. Now set the shoes aside to let the plaster dry while you clean up the mess.

Remember, *never* pour any leftover plaster of Paris into the sink! Soak up water and plaster with newspapers and finish up with paper towels; dispose in the garbage.

Within half an hour you will feel the heat of the plaster. Don't worry as it won't get hot enough to burn you; but this does indicate hardening or setting up. In about two hours the plaster will feel firm enough to proceed.

3. Removing Lasts

Begin cutting around the sole of the shoe, on the *upper*, and cut stitching in back seam, using your utility knife as shown in Figures 4 a, b, and c. Cut the entire *upper* away from the sole. Lift out the plaster of Paris *last* (see Figure 5).

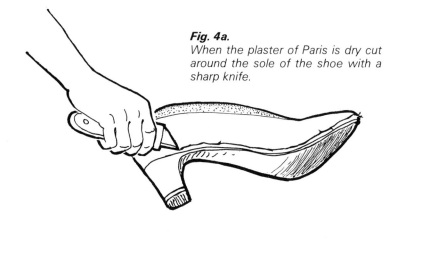

Fig. 4a.
When the plaster of Paris is dry cut around the sole of the shoe with a sharp knife.

Fig. 4b.
Slit the back seam of the upper.

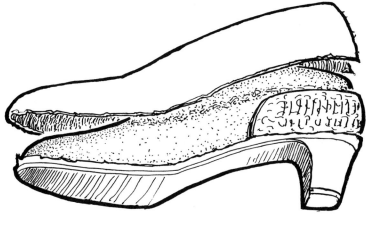

Fig. 4c.
The entire upper is cut away from the shoe. Note that the counter will probably remain attached to the heel and will require a screwdriver, hammer, and pliers to remove from the heel.

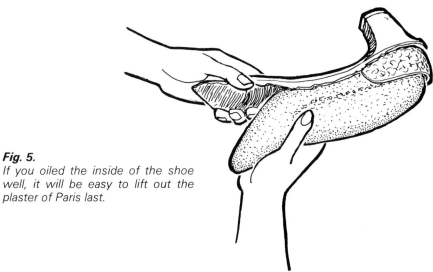

Fig. 5.
If you oiled the inside of the shoe well, it will be easy to lift out the plaster of Paris last.

Smooth off the rough edges of the lasts with a metal vegetable scraper, metal sandpaper, or knife as illustrated in Figure 6. If a ridge forms on the top edge of the *lasts*, remove this too with coarse sandpaper. Look for air holes or dents in the plaster. You can mix a bit of plaster and water to fill the holes.

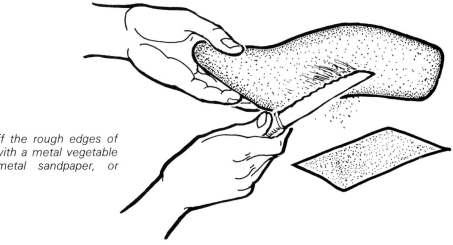

Fig. 6.
Smooth off the rough edges of the lasts with a metal vegetable scraper, metal sandpaper, or knife.

With a screwdriver, hammer, and pliers take the rest of the shoes apart (see Figure 7). The factory-made shoes contain many little nails; pull them out and remove the *counter.* Remove the coverings on the heels. *Do not throw any pieces of the shoes away!* Store all parts of the shoes—no matter how messy—in a box for later reference.

Fig. 7.
Using a screwdriver, hammer, and pliers—and a bit of determination—take the rest of the shoe apart.

Trace around the heavy innersole from the shoe onto a heavy piece of cardboard. Shape the cardboard under the arch so that it will fit next to your last as shown in Figure 8. Some cardboard has a "grain" so it rolls in one direction and makes a sharp crease in the other.

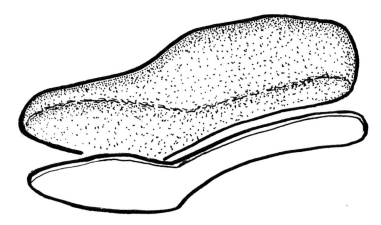

Fig. 8.
Glue a piece of cardboard the shape of the innersole to the bottom of the last.

Glue the cardboard in place on the bottom of your lasts with white glue. Slip each last into the toe of a nylon stocking and pull it tightly by tying the top into a knot as shown in Figures 9a and b. Plaster of Paris has a very dry feeling, and the stocking prevents the new uppers from sticking to the last.

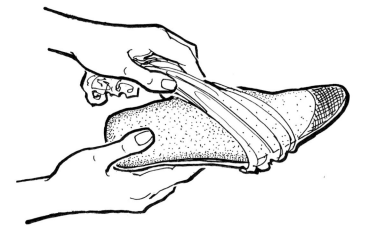

Fig. 9a.
Slip each last into the toe of a nylon stocking.

Fig. 9b.
Tie the stockings into a knot and cut off tops.

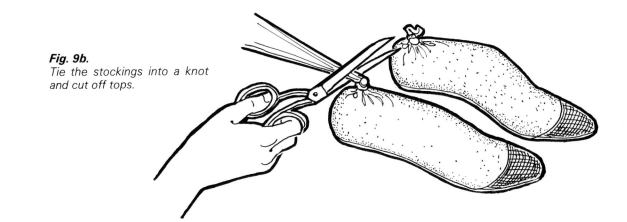

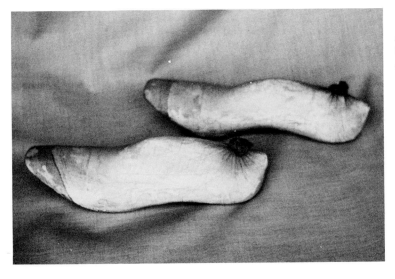

A finished pair of lasts with their stocking coverings (see Figure 9b).

You can expect to make some adjustments on the lasts for a more accurate fit after you make the first pair of shoes. To achieve the perfect fit and individualize your lasts, remove the stockings and either scrape away some of the plaster in the places you want the shoe tighter or add a bit of plaster to make the shoe larger.

From these lasts you can make any number of shoes. Fashion will only change the shape of the toe or the heel. With my own favorite lasts I have created pointed, squared, and rounded toes. The actual fit of the shoe measures from the ball of the foot to the heel. This part remains the same regardless of fashion.

4. Adjusting the Toes

When fashion indicates a change, I alter the shape of the toes by the following procedure:

Trace the shape of the bottoms of your lasts from the ball of the foot forward on a heavy piece of cardboard. Do this for each last as illustrated in Figure 10. Draft a new toe shape over these lines (see Figures 11a and b). Then cut the two cardboard shapes along the new lines.

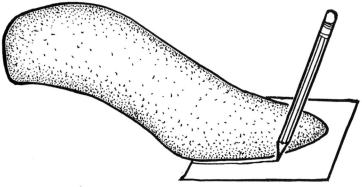

Fig. 10.
Trace the outline of the toe of the last onto cardboard.

Fig. 11a.
Draw a new shape for the toe of the last.

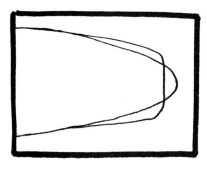

Fig. 11b.
Cut out cardboard on the new lines.

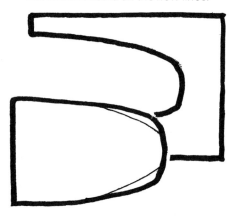

To create a new toe shape, glue these pieces of cardboard to the bottoms of your lasts as shown in Figure 12. If the old contour of the toe extends over the edges of your new shape, cut or sand off the excess plaster. When you extend the new shape to fill in the new line, mix a little plaster and water so you can shape the new toes with your fingers as described in Figures 13a and b. Follow the same method of mixing the plaster when you made the last except you can mix this small amount in a cup. When the new plaster dries, sand it smooth and carefully peel away the cardboard pattern. Remember to change the shape of your innersole and sole patterns to match the new one.

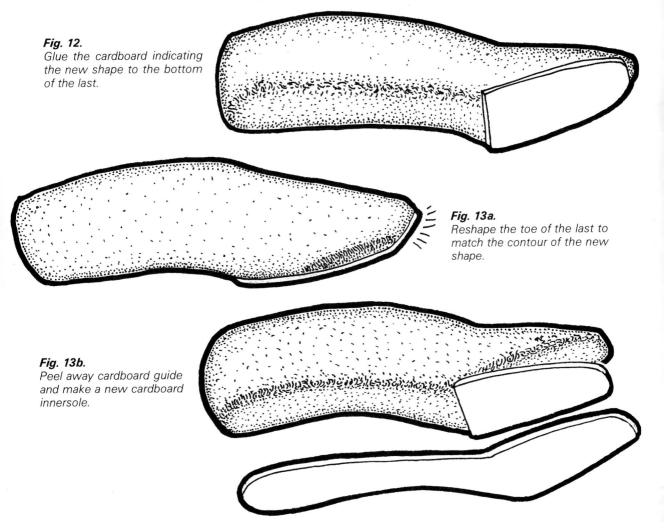

Fig. 12.
Glue the cardboard indicating the new shape to the bottom of the last.

Fig. 13a.
Reshape the toe of the last to match the contour of the new shape.

Fig. 13b.
Peel away cardboard guide and make a new cardboard innersole.

If you wish, you can make a pair of shoes on your new lasts before they dry completely. They need weeks to dry thoroughly, so store them in a place where they will get some ventilation. When you put them away in a closed box, they will mildew. In case this happens, mix ¼ cup bleach to one gallon water and soak them for a half hour or until clean.

III

CUSTOM-MADE LASTS

CASTING YOUR FEET If you have a particular foot problem or want truly custom-fit to your shoes, you can make lasts from casting your feet. With this project you will need a friend to help you.

1. Materials to Have at Hand

[handwritten: pencil, tape, friend, innersole, glue, knife, ruler]

Several days newspapers for spreading out on the floor.

Ten pounds of plaster of Paris.

Two pairs of old nylon stockings.

½ cup oil or Vaseline for greasing the feet.

Two large plastic bowls, 2 quart capacity; one for mixing the plaster and the other for washing the hands.

Two heels from an old pair of shoes—the height heel you wish to make your new shoes.

Two pieces of medium-weight cardboard, 4 by 10 inches, to make a little "ramp" to lift your toes.

Medium size screwdriver and a hammer.

Two shoe boxes, or boxes of that size to contain the plaster.

2. Casting the Feet

Choose a pair of heels the height you want for your shoes and fasten them to the bottom of the two boxes near one end. Place them in a position where you can stand on the heels and secure them with tape or put clay around them. (Make sure the heels lay flat on the bottom of the box.) Don't put the clay *under* the heels, or this will alter the height. Set your foot on the heel and mark where the ball of the foot rests (see Figures 14a and b). Make a *"ramp"* of the cardboard and tape it into place so that it makes your toes turn up slightly.

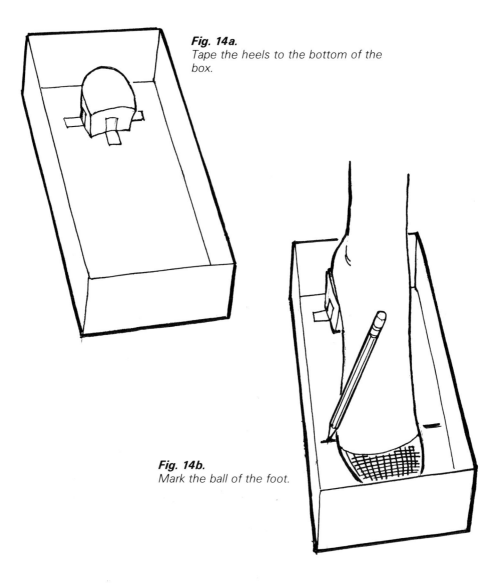

Fig. 14a.
Tape the heels to the bottom of the box.

Fig. 14b.
Mark the ball of the foot.

Put *two* nylon stockings on *each* foot to restrict and smooth the contour of the foot. Grease or oil them thoroughly. While sitting in a chair with the boxes on the floor in front of you, place each foot on the heels in the boxes. Make sure the "ramp" lifts the toes as shown in Figure 15.

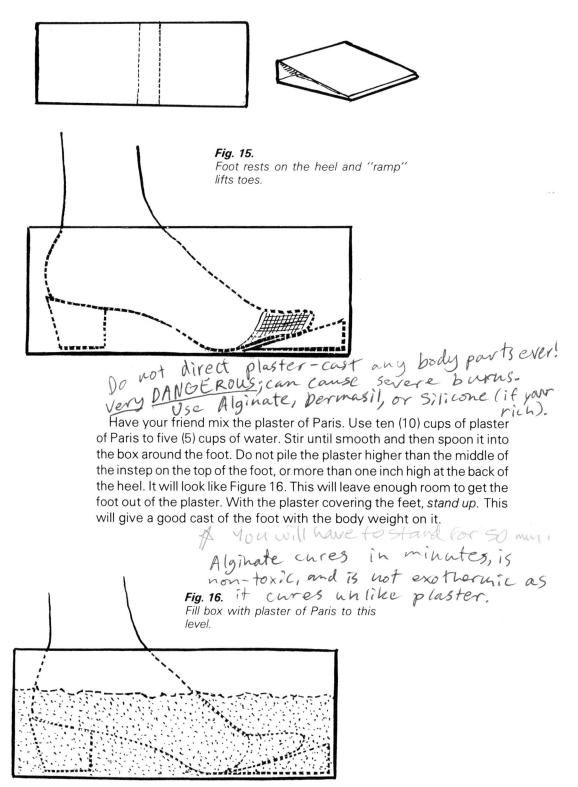

Fig. 15.
*Foot rests on the heel and "ramp"
lifts toes.*

*Do not direct plaster-cast any body parts ever!
Very DANGEROUS; can cause severe burns.
Use Alginate, Dermasil, or Silicone (if your
rich).*

Have your friend mix the plaster of Paris. Use ten (10) cups of plaster of Paris to five (5) cups of water. Stir until smooth and then spoon it into the box around the foot. Do not pile the plaster higher than the middle of the instep on the top of the foot, or more than one inch high at the back of the heel. It will look like Figure 16. This will leave enough room to get the foot out of the plaster. With the plaster covering the feet, *stand up.* This will give a good cast of the foot with the body weight on it.

*# You will have to stand for 50 min.
Alginate cures in minutes, is
non-toxic, and is not exothermic as
it cures unlike plaster.*

Fig. 16.
*Fill box with plaster of Paris to this
level.*

a lot of

In about half an hour the setting up process of the plaster causes heat. Don't panic! The plaster will ~~not get~~ hot enough to cause ~~any~~ discomfort. When the heat subsides—perhaps another twenty minutes, you can remove your feet.

3. Removing the Feet from the Plaster

Sit down and relax your feet. Gently pull your feet out of the plaster. One nylon stocking will remain inside the mold, and the other will come out with your foot. You can pull the stockings out of the plaster mold after you remove your feet. Now you have a *negative* mold of your feet. Let these negative molds dry at least a day before proceeding to the next step (see Figure 17).

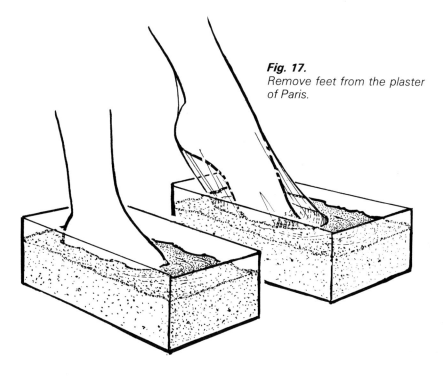

Fig. 17.
Remove feet from the plaster of Paris.

4. Making the Positive Casts

Thoroughly oil the insides of these molds with about ⅛ cup oil for each one. Tip the boxes if necessary so that you get the oil spread around. Pour out any excess oil. Mix two (2) cups water and four (4) cups plaster of Paris in one of your plastic bowls. When you have stirred it until it is smooth carefully spoon it into the toe area. Tap the bottom of the box to make bubbles rise, then fill entire holes. Do put the molds aside for a day or so to thoroughly dry before continuing (see Figures 18a and b).

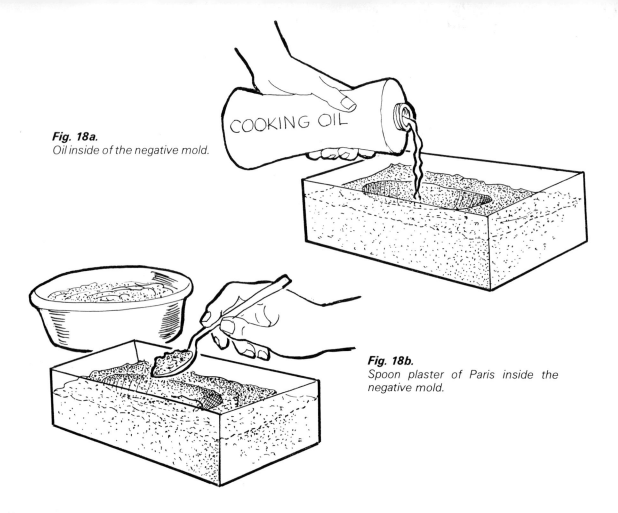

Fig. 18a.
Oil inside of the negative mold.

Fig. 18b.
Spoon plaster of Paris inside the negative mold.

Spread newspapers over an area of at least five (5) feet square. Peel the cardboard boxes from the plaster. Place the screwdriver on the top of the *negative* mold, the first plaster you poured over the feet. Gentle taps with a hammer will separate the plaster from the *positive* molds of your feet because of the oiled insides (see illustration in Figure 19).

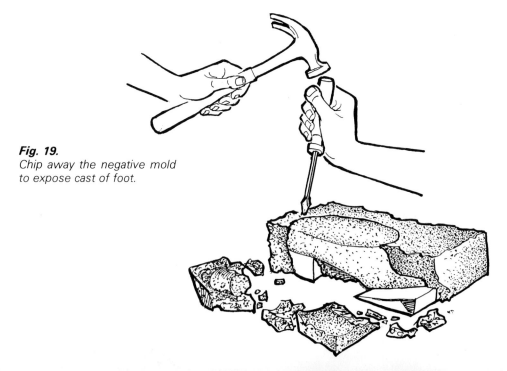

Fig. 19.
Chip away the negative mold to expose cast of foot.

When you have chipped away all the plaster from the negative mold, the two casts of your feet remain. Now you must make them "shoe-shaped."

5. Making "Lasts" from Your "Casts"

Trace the innersole patterns from a pair of your shoes onto a piece of medium-weight cardboard. Cut these out and glue them to the bottoms of your "casts." You can use white glue for this. These shapes will give you a guide to contour the "shoe shapes."

Shoes always measure narrower than the foot itself, so you will want to restrict the foot and yet make the shoe comfortable and roomy. All pumps extend beyond the toes at least one-half inch so you will need to build a toe-room area on the end of the last. If you made a pair of lasts from a pair of shoes, you will have an idea of the shape you want to attain.

Build up the heel area and the top of the instep by adding plaster a spoonful at a time. As the plaster hardens, it builds easily.

Carve and shape on the plaster with long strokes down the sides. So that you will make both lasts the same, count the strokes you take on each one. If you took ten strokes on the outside of one last, then take ten strokes on the other last in the corresponding place. Scoop out the arch to make it higher if you wish.

Shave or scrape the toe area with a knife to remove any bumps. Use your hands to form a smooth last, dipping them into your washing bowl frequently. Follow the instructions in Figures 20a, b, c, d, e, and f.

How to deal with unusual foot features?

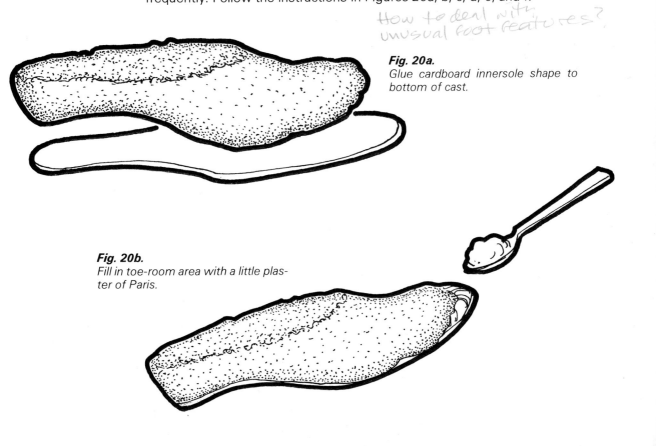

Fig. 20a.
Glue cardboard innersole shape to bottom of cast.

Fig. 20b.
Fill in toe-room area with a little plaster of Paris.

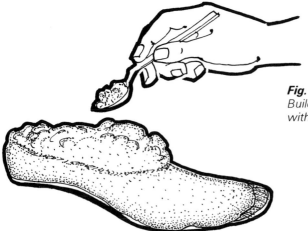

Fig. 20c.
Build up heel area and top of instep with plaster of Paris.

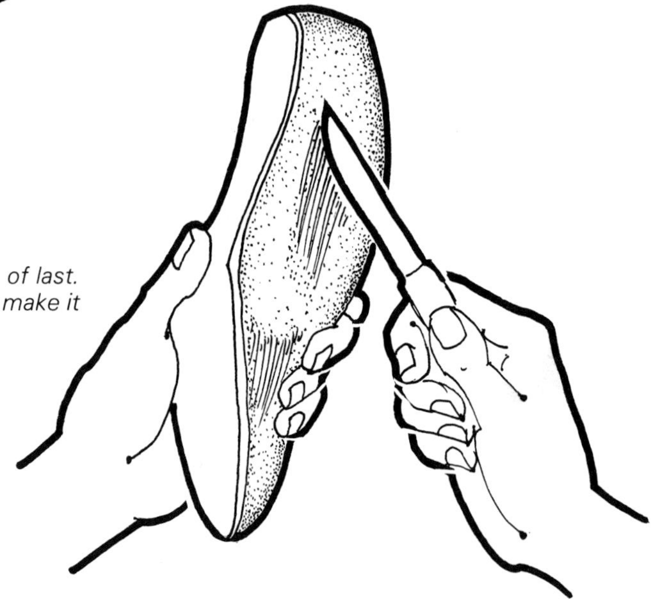

Fig. 20d.
Carve and shape sides of last. Scoop out arch area to make it higher.

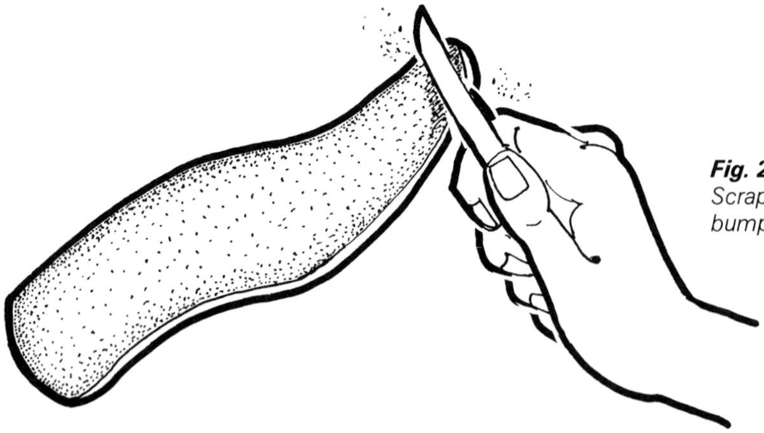

Fig. 20e.
Scrape toe area to remove any bumps.

Fig. 20f.
Smooth the last with wet hands.

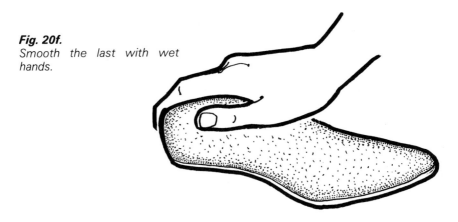

Slip each last into a nylon stocking and pull it tightly by tying the top into a knot as shown in Figure 21.

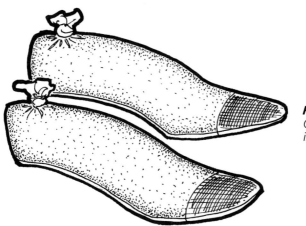

Fig. 21.
Cover lasts with nylon stockings.

Save the heels you used for making the casts of your feet; they will be your master pattern for the heel height for your new shoes.

Now you have made the lasts; we will make your patterns.

IV
PATTERN
DRAFTING

Let's begin by making a set of patterns for a basic pump. Later you may restyle the pattern for your upper exactly as you would create new patterns from your basic dress pattern.

You will make three patterns for the upper of the shoe: one for the outer fabric, muslin interlining, and the felt or leather lining, and two patterns for the buckram reinforcing.

BASIC PATTERNS If you have made your lasts from a pair of shoes, soak the upper in water until thoroughly wet and flatten it to make a pattern. Lay the upper on a piece of cardboard or heavy paper and trace around it adding ⅜ inch at the back seam edge for an allowance and one inch all around the outer edge as pictured in Figure 22. Extend the front of the pattern to a point so that you can use it as a guide in centering your fabrics.

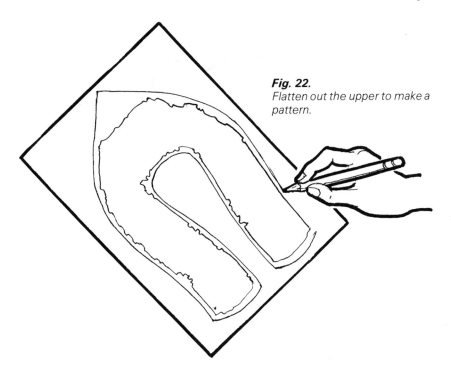

Fig. 22.
Flatten out the upper to make a pattern.

Make patterns of all parts of the shoe you used to make your last as illustrated in Figure 23.

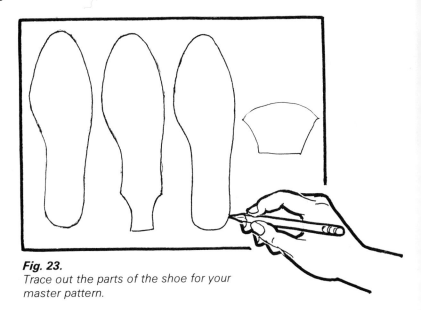

Fig. 23.
Trace out the parts of the shoe for your master pattern.

If you made a set of lasts from your feet, use the pattern graph shown in Figure 24. This pattern includes seam allowances. The manager of a large shoe store pointed out, ''The most common size is 7½. Each full size differs $3/16$ inch." I have outlined the "$7\frac{1}{2}$." Each square represents one square inch. Enlarge or decrease the graph to make your size according to the diagram in Figure 25.

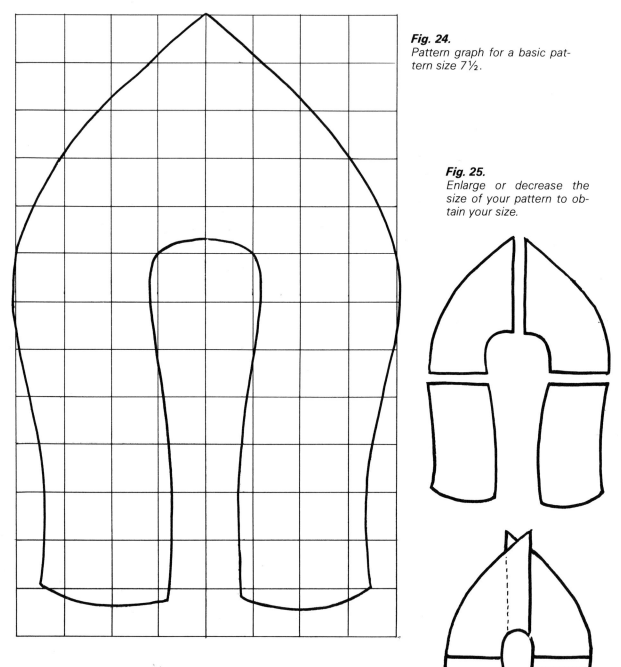

Fig. 24.
Pattern graph for a basic pattern size $7\frac{1}{2}$.

Fig. 25.
Enlarge or decrease the size of your pattern to obtain your size.

This will not fit a foot that differs from the norm.

1. Drafting Your Patterns

Trace your basic pattern onto a piece of heavy paper or lightweight cardboard. Label this first pattern A. Trace pattern A on a piece of heavy paper or on lightweight cardboard and cut it ⅛ inch smaller around the inside edge. Label this pattern B. Trace pattern B onto heavy paper or cardboard and alter it ⅛ inch smaller around the inside edge. Trim ⅛ inch off from the pattern. Label it pattern C.

Each pattern is "stepped-off" in size to eliminate bulky double edges of buckram around the edge on top of the shoes as described in Figures 26a, b, c, and d.

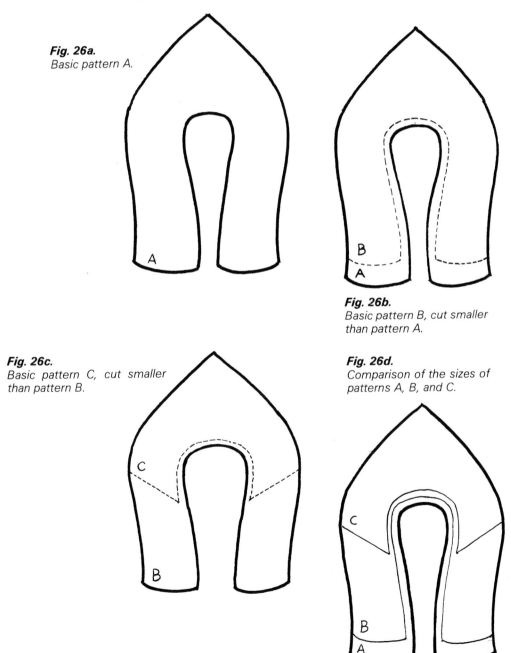

Fig. 26a.
Basic pattern A.

Fig. 26b.
Basic pattern B, cut smaller than pattern A.

Fig. 26c.
Basic pattern C, cut smaller than pattern B.

Fig. 26d.
Comparison of the sizes of patterns A, B, and C.

2. Label Your Patterns

Make the following notations on these patterns:

Pattern A. Cut muslin pattern always on the straight of the goods. This also serves as the lining pattern for felt or lightweight leather. Leather or felt has no warp or woof so you can cut in any direction. *Never cut out the center of this pattern in the outer fabric, muslin interlining, or lining* until *after* you sew the seam on the pattern line.

Pattern B. Cut from buckram on the bias.

Pattern C. Cut from buckram on the straight of the goods. By using two thicknesses of buckram with different directions of grain, you strengthen the shape of the shoe's toe area.

These patterns are the same for right and left! The uppers automatically become right and left shaped when you wet and form the uppers onto the lasts. The same pattern also works for a high or low heeled shoe.

3. Styles

You, like others I have taught, will soon make a low, medium, and high heel set of lasts to accent your wardrobe.

Clip and file pictures of interesting shoe styles from newspapers and magazines. In chapter XII on Sandals you will find information on making straps and duplicating patterns. See chapter X under "Heels" for further information about taking factory-made shoes apart.

Occasionally when a friend wears a pair of shoes with an interesting pattern, I ask her to give them to me when she wears them out. I take *one* of the shoes apart, make a set of patterns using my basic pattern to adjust for size, and keep the other shoe for a model of the finished product. Then I make a pair of shoes on my lasts, using the new pattern.

Let's now construct the complete uppers from patterns A, B, and C.

V
CONSTRUCTING
THE UPPERS

Almost any fabric will form the outer part of the uppers. The inner construction remains the same for all types of shoes. The buckram inside the shoes shapes and strengthens the uppers. I prefer to work with wool, cotton, or linen in a medium-weight fabric for the outer material. These fabrics make the work easy and assure you of good results, especially for a beginner.

Before proceeding see chapter XI for a discussion on the various fabrics you can use for making the uppers.

I have chosen a red wool plaid for the outer material of the shoes as a demonstration. Choose your fabric and let's make a pair of uppers together.

Before proceeding see chapter X for information on muslin, buckram, and felt.

1. Combining the Muslin and Buckram

Trace pattern A onto a piece of muslin or lightweight plain colored cotton fabric. This is the *interlining* of the upper. Use a ball-point pen with a *clean* line. Make two tracings of this pattern on the straight of the goods. You do not need to reverse the pattern for the second tracing because both uppers are identical until they are formed onto the lasts. Cut around the outer edge, but leave the center solid as shown in Figure 27.

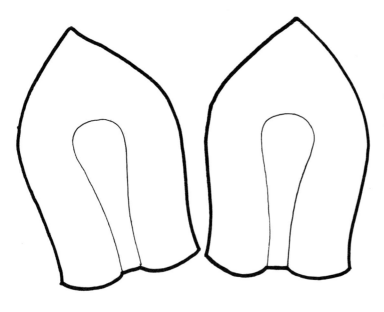

Fig. 27.
Cut two pieces of muslin from pattern A, leaving centers uncut.

Cut pattern B from heavy uniform fiber buckram on the bias.
Cut pattern C from heavy uniform fiber buckram on the straight.
See Figure 28.

Fig. 28.
Cut pattern B from bias buckram; pattern C from buckram on the straight.

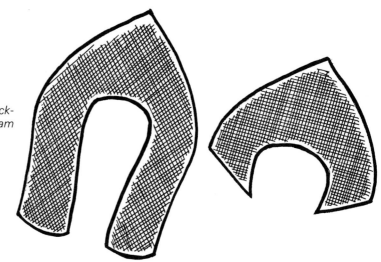

Sew pattern C to pattern B as shown in Figure 29.

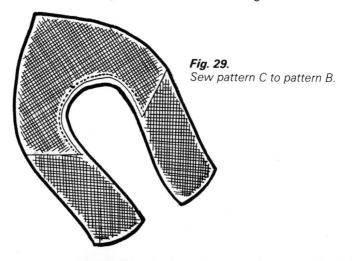

Fig. 29.
Sew pattern C to pattern B.

Sew pattern B, with pattern C attached, to pattern A (see Figure 30). If your thread breaks when you sew through the buckram, try adjusting the tension on the top thread and change to a larger size needle. If the buckram curls and is difficult to stitch, iron the buckram flat to the muslin. Spray a little water on the back of the buckram on pattern B, with pattern C attached, but only enough to dampen or stick the buckram to the muslin when you iron it. Experiment with a scrap of buckram and muslin to determine exactly how much you need to dampen the buckram. Don't wet the buckram too much as it will distort your pattern shape before you sew it together. When you stick the buckram patterns B and C to pattern A, you will find stitching them together an easy task.

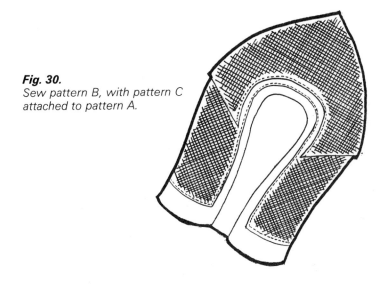

Fig. 30.
Sew pattern B, with pattern C attached to pattern A.

2. Cutting the Outer Fabric for the Upper

Since I am using a plaid fabric for this pair of pumps, the design of each shoe must match exactly. The slightest difference in placement of the pattern would make the shoes look mismatched.

Pin the back of pattern A muslin to the wrong side of your fabric. To find the right spot, scotch-tape the outer fabric up to a window so that the light will enable you to see the pattern of the fabric. When you have determined the exact same position on each upper, place several pins through the center of the muslin and fabric to hold the position. The point at the end of your basic pattern acts as a center guide.

In placing your pattern on the fabric keep in mind the vamp of your shoe extends approximately 2 to 2½ inches and the outer part of your pattern disappears in the sole of the shoe.

3. Sewing the Uppers

With patterns A, B, and C pinned in place onto the *wrong* side of the outer fabric, place this, right side of fabric down, on your lining. If you are using a leather for lining, you will place it onto the smooth side of the leather. Felt does not have a right or wrong side.

Sew along the ball-point pen marking on pattern A muslin. Begin your stitching 1 ½ inches in from the back seam on the other side. Do not lock your sewing with a backstitch.

Fig. 31.
Sew muslin pattern A to outer fabric and lining.

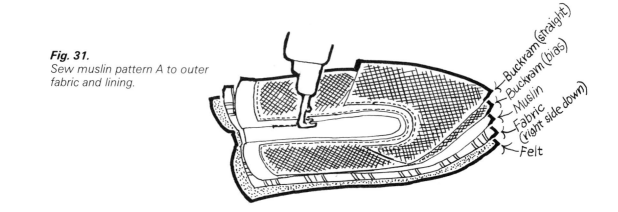

Buckram (straight)
Buckram (bias)
Muslin
Fabric (right side down)
Felt

Sewing the upper together as detailed in Figure 31.

Before you cut out the center, lift the layers and check your stitching. In case you did not stitch exactly where you marked, you may rip your stitches and make a correction.

Cut straight into the center for approximately 2 inches, then continue snipping around the inside ⅛ inch from your stitching, as shown in

Figure 32. Trim outer edge and back seam edge even with the muslin pattern A.

Fig. 32.
Cut and trim the center of the upper.

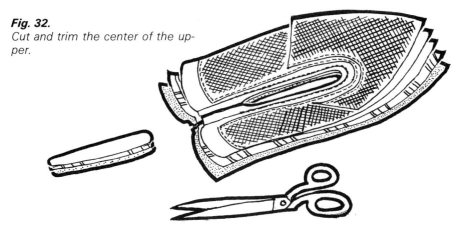

Turn the upper right side out. With the felt side up, pull the outer fabric into the center and stitch ⅛ inch from the edge seam, beginning approximately 2 inches from the back seam edge. Catch all layers *except* the outer fabric (see Figure 33). This stitching will require a bit of practice, but it will prevent the edge of your upper from "rolling." This functions very much like the understitching on a neck facing or collar.

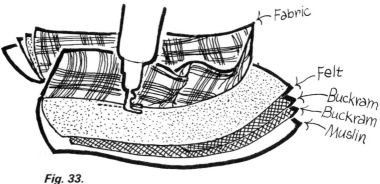

Fig. 33.
Topstitch lining to the muslin to prevent "rolling."

Make the back seam in two sections; first seam the muslin and outer fabric together (see Figure 34). Then sew the lining in a separate seam. Retain the curve in the seams. *Pull the lining into place and connect the top seam on the ball-point pen line*, overlapping ½ inch the existing stitches sewed in Figure 31 (see Figure 35). Carefully trim away excess fabric to ⅛ inch and notch the back seam of muslin and outer fabric. Do not notch the felt seam (see Figure 36).

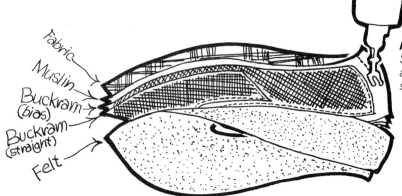

Fabric
Muslin
Buckram (bias)
Buckram (straight)
Felt

Fig. 34.
Stitch back seam, catching muslin and outer fabric. Sew lining back seam separately.

Sewing the back seam of the upper (see Figure 34).

Fig. 35.
Connect the line of stitching sewed in Figure 31.

Fig. 36.
Trim and notch back seam.

Now you are ready to form the uppers onto your lasts.

VI
FORMING
THE UPPERS
ONTO THE LASTS

I always consider my shoes half finished when I reach this point. Now the entire process becomes handwork, which you do at your leisure. I like to save this particular step for "evening work." You need less concentration to do the hand sewing than the machine work in chapter V.

Collect the following materials for this next step in your shoemaking: medium size Turkish towel, nylon yarn, large needle, thimble, scissors, pliers, small sponge, counters, concentrated laundry starch, and your lasts, as illustrated in Figure 37.

Before proceeding see chapter X on purchasing materials.

1. Wetting the Upper

Separate the layers of fabrics and dampen the buckram and felt with water using a sponge or your fingertips. Wet the buckram only enough to make it pliable. Separate the two layers of buckram and rub about a tablespoonful of concentrated liquid laundry starch, full strength, into the toe area near the vamp, as shown in Figure 38. This will reinforce the stiffening of the buckram in the toe area. Wash your hands to remove the sticky starch so you won't soil the outer fabric. If you do happen to get some starch on the fabric, remove it with a damp cloth.

Fig. 37.
Materials used in forming the uppers onto the lasts.

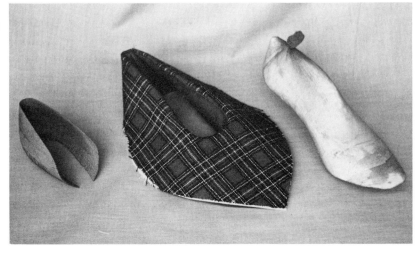

Counter, upper, and last (see Figure 37).

Fig. 38.
Rub concentrated laundry starch into the toe area for reinforcing.

When the upper feels limp and pliable, insert the counter inside the back of the upper. The lining will be on the inside of the counter and the muslin interlining and outer fabric will surround the outside of the counter as illustrated in Figure 39. Be sure to line up the center back seam of the upper perfectly with the "seam" on the back of the counter. Inspect the counter closely to find that center "seam" as it is often difficult to find on some.

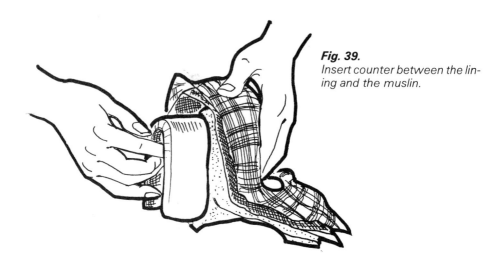

Fig. 39.
Insert counter between the lining and the muslin.

2. Putting the Upper onto the Last

Insert the last inside the upper, heel first, so as to fit snugly into the counter as shown in Figure 40. Figure 41 shows the felt lining visible below the counter and the other fabrics surrounding the outside of the counter. Turn the work over and begin to form the upper by pulling forward and down at the sides of the last, gripping it securely at the area of the ball of the foot as shown in Figure 42.

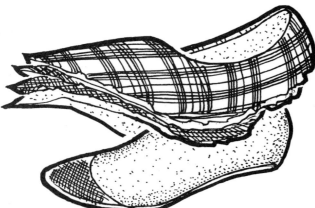

Fig. 40.
Set the last into the counter area of the upper.

Fig. 41.
Lining is visible on bottom below the counter and the outer material surrounds the counter.

Fig. 42.
Stretch all material forward and down at the ball of the foot.

Upper placed onto the last (see Figure 42).

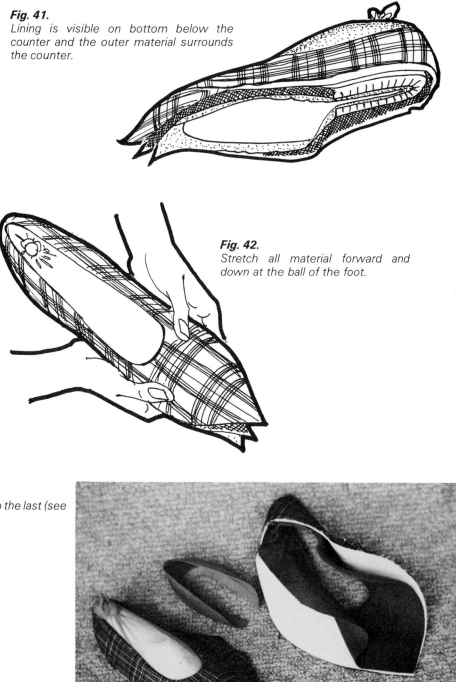

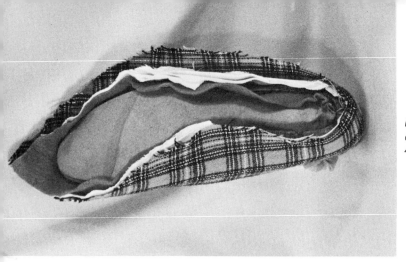

Upper placed onto the last showing detail of the bottom (see also Figure 41).

With a large needle threaded with a single strand of nylon yarn, sew at the ball of the foot and stitch from side to side, across the bottom of the last, pulling the yarn tightly, catching all layers and molding the shoe as you go. Turn work over and pull up the layers to inspect for a hidden wrinkle. Pull each layer separately beginning with the felt to remove all wrinkles. Each layer must fit smoothly (see Figures 43a and b).

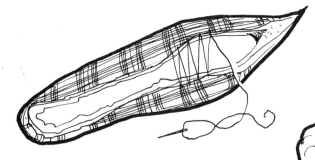

Fig. 43a.
Hand stitch from side to side, molding the upper to the last.

Fig. 43b.
Pull each layer separately to remove hidden wrinkles.

Forming the upper onto the last (see Figures 42 and 43).

Turn the last over occasionally and check for balance of placement on the last. Make any corrections. Check the back seam alignment in the center of the shoe. If not centered, remove the upper from the last and replace the counter into the upper. I have made shoes with the back seam a bit off on one shoe. It really bothers me after I finished and realized I should have corrected it when I formed the upper on the last. I remember going to a party and reminding myself which shoe contained the *straight* back seam so that I could take that shoe off for anyone to inspect!

Now that you have centered your back seam, you can continue sewing the upper onto the last.

If you smooth the materials on the *top* of the shoe, don't worry about the bottom. Pull the yarn over the toe to hold the fabrics into position as shown in Figure 44. You may find much excess material, especially at the bottom of the toe of the shoe. This will be snipped away later when the upper is dry.

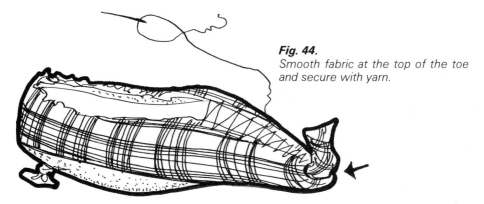

Fig. 44.
Smooth fabric at the top of the toe and secure with yarn.

Continue forming and stitching the upper to the last by sewing back and forth with nylon yarn. From time to time go back over the existing stitches and tighten them if they have loosened.

When you reach the counter area, pull the felt with pliers. Stretch the felt from side to side to remove any hidden folds in the lining as shown in Figure 45. Now trim away the excess felt stretched beyond the counter.

Fig. 45.
Pull lining with pliers to remove any hidden folds.

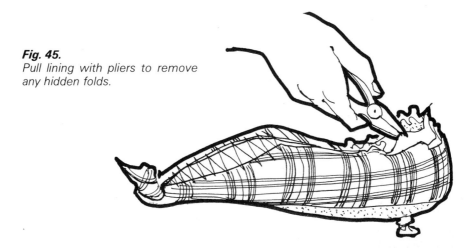

Do not try to sew through the counter; it isn't necessary and the needle probably wouldn't sew through it. Smooth the outer fabric over the counter and catch only the outer fabric and the muslin in your stitches. Do not pull your stitches too tightly over the counter, or you expose the lining around the top of the counter area.

Finish by tightening the area along the instep. Keep your stitches close to the center of the arch in the bottom of the shoe so that no stitch holes will show on the finished shoe (see Figures 46a and b).

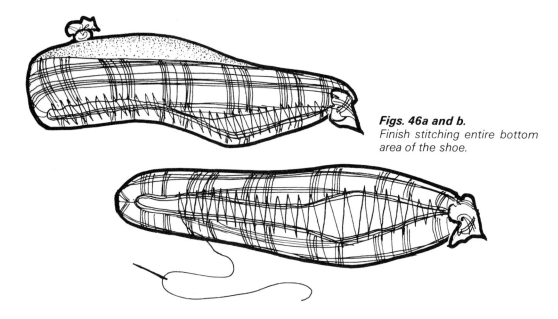

Figs. 46a and b.
Finish stitching entire bottom area of the shoe.

Sewing the upper onto the last (see Figure 46).

Close-up of the upper sewed onto the last (see Figure 46).

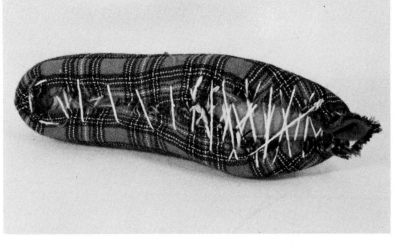

3. Drying the Uppers

Wrap the counter area of each shoe with a piece of white cloth, approximately 18 inches long and 2 inches wide, as shown in Figure 47. Old sheeting works fine. Keep firm but never *tight* and secure the end of the strip of sheeting with a straight pin, either into the bottom of the shoe or into the nylon stocking at the top of the last. Never pin into the side of the shoe as it will create a hole in the fabric.

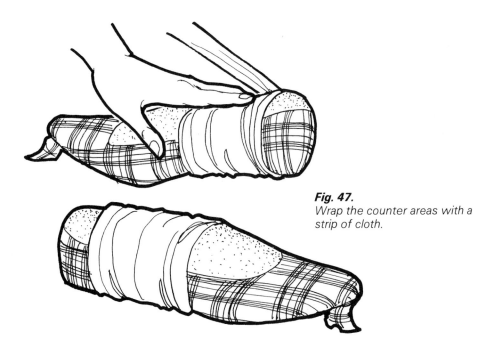

Fig. 47.
Wrap the counter areas with a strip of cloth.

This wrapping encourages the counter to dry closely to the last and hold the shape.

You may dry your shoes in the oven at a low temperature (250 degrees). Generally, an hour will dry them thoroughly; however, the time will depend on whether you started with a thoroughly dry last, how wet you made the upper, or the type of fabric you chose. Set the timer and check the shoes quite often during the drying if you put them in the oven. Don't scorch your shoes!

To dry them naturally, place the lasts and uppers in a well-ventilated spot, perhaps near a window. Avoid a sunny spot as they could fade. They will need at least a day to dry naturally.

Occasionally, I have placed the lasts with uppers on them into the toes of nylon stockings and hung them on the line in the shade or in the house near a heat vent. Perhaps you can improvise another way for drying your shoes!

To test for dryness, cut a few of the nylon stitches and feel inside. When the uppers feel perfectly dry, you prepare to remove them from the lasts.

VII
REMOVING
THE UPPERS
FROM THE LASTS

Snip your hand stitching on the bottoms of the lasts. Most of these stitches you will cut away, so don't bother to pull them out. When you have cut all the stitches holding the uppers onto the lasts, open the toe area at the bottom of the last. Don't worry about bending the buckram at the *bottom* of the toe as it will snap back into position if thoroughly dry. Gently work the last out of the upper, toe first as shown in Figures 48a, b, and c. If it sticks, check to see if a stitch has caught onto the stocking covering.

   The last should "pop" out of the bottom. Don't force the upper from the last but gently work the last out. Your shoe will retain a stiff form until after you attach the sole. Later, the sides of the shoes will soften a little with wear.

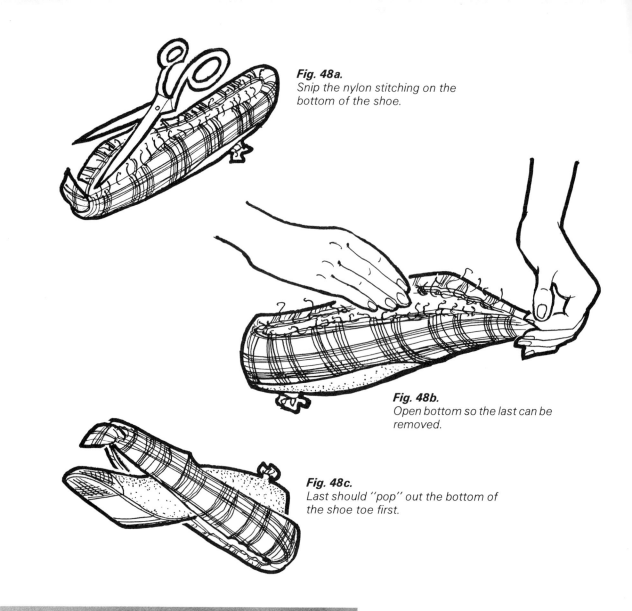

Fig. 48a.
Snip the nylon stitching on the bottom of the shoe.

Fig. 48b.
Open bottom so the last can be removed.

Fig. 48c.
Last should "pop" out the bottom of the shoe toe first.

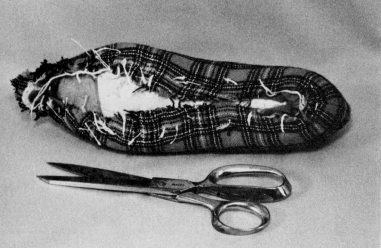

Stitches are cut after the upper is dry (see Figure 48a).

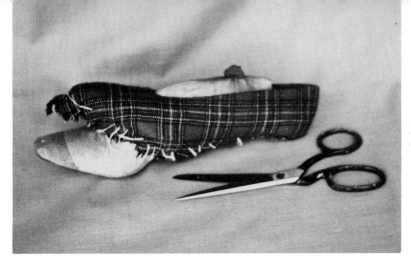

Last will "pop" out the bottom of the upper when dry.

1. Cutting Away Excess Fabric

Make a chalk mark ½ inch from the edge of the bottom of the shoe as illustrated in Figure 49. This line will guide you in cutting away the excess fabric. I use my leather scissors for this project as they simplify the job.

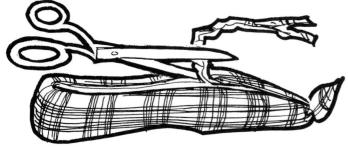

Fig. 49.
Make a chalk mark ½ inch in from the outer edge of shoe.

Trim away the stitch area and leave ½ inch of the shoe to extend under the sole. To remove most of the lumps and folds from the bottoms, make notches to remove any remaining folds as shown in Figure 50. Don't notch too close to the outside edge of the shoe.

Fig. 50.
Trim away center excess fabric at the chalk mark.

Lift back the *outer material* from the toe area and cut away *muslin, buckram, both layers, and the felt lining* in the toe area. Cut off these fabrics at the sole level and leave only the outer fabric to extend under the sole to form a neat toe (see Figure 51).

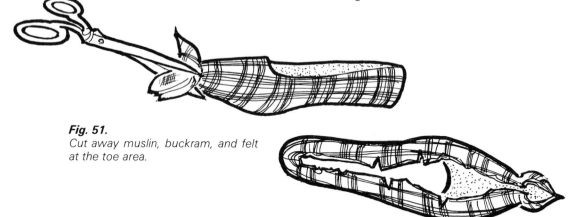

Fig. 51.
Cut away muslin, buckram, and felt at the toe area.

While you trim the upper, handle it carefully so you don't bend it out of shape. In case you make shoes of a very thin outer fabric, do not cut off the muslin interlining at the bottom of the toe.

2. Making the Innersole

Most factory-made shoes contain a very heavy innersole, but you don't need one for handmade shoes. The heavy innersole provides firmness for nailing the heel. Since you substitute shoemakers' cement instead of nails to assemble the *entire shoe*, you can dispense with heavy innersoles. Heavy cardboard innersoles will hold the uppers in shape so you can continue to assemble the shoes.

Cut two cardboard innersoles using a pattern made from the shape of the bottom of the last. Copy this contour accurately as these innersoles keep your shoes in the proper shape. "Roll" the cardboard in the arch section and insert into the upper as shown in Figures 52a and b.

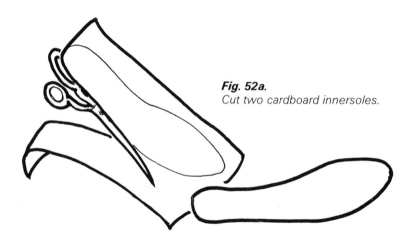

Fig. 52a.
Cut two cardboard innersoles.

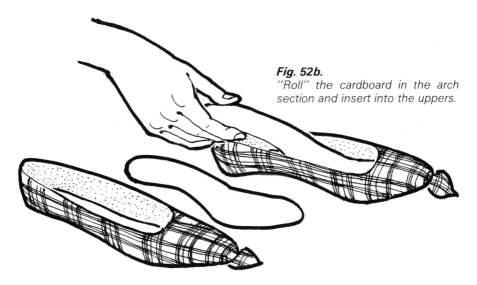

Fig. 52b.
"Roll" the cardboard in the arch section and insert into the uppers.

3. Working with Shoemakers' Cement

Here are some tips on working with this cement. First of all, work in a well-ventilated room. It is flammable so do not smoke around the cement. Keep the top covered as it will evaporate quickly.

The cement runs and acts very much like honey so learn to control it so you don't dribble onto your work. In case you get a spot of cement on your fabric, you can sometimes remove it by making a "ball" of nearly dry cement and rub it on the stain to "erase" it. Sometimes you can find a little ball of the cement around the top of the can.

Working from the bottom, apply shoemakers' cement to the cardboard and felt in the ½ inch area of the upper which extends under the sole (see Figure 53). Apply some cement into the loose areas around the counter. I keep one hand inside the shoe, pushing the cardboard down onto the felt while working. Apply some cement on the flap of the outer fabric under the toe of the shoe as shown in Figure 54.

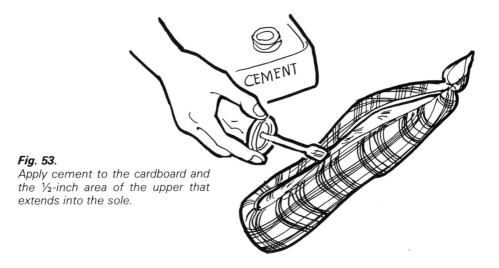

Fig. 53.
Apply cement to the cardboard and the ½-inch area of the upper that extends into the sole.

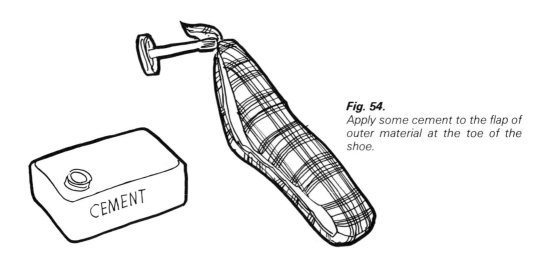

Fig. 54.
Apply some cement to the flap of outer material at the toe of the shoe.

The cemented parts will not stick together until dry. In about 15 minutes you can press all the edges flat on the sole. Before sticking down the fabric on the toe, place a small piece of felt or other padding onto the cardboard innersole in the area where buckram and felt were cut away (see Figure 55). This will act as a "filler" and prevent the toe from depressing.

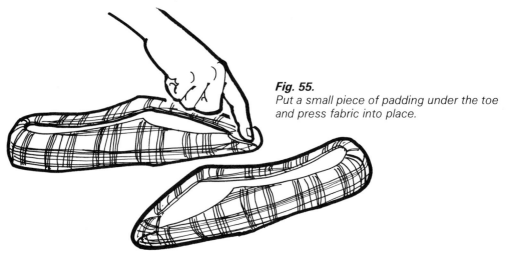

Fig. 55.
Put a small piece of padding under the toe and press fabric into place.

Cut and cement into place pieces of padding into the areas of the sole and heel as pictured in Figure 56. Do not pad the arch section.

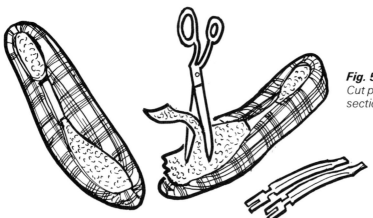

Fig. 56.
Cut padding to fit sole and heel section and cement into place.

Bottom of shoe is padded and shank is cemented into place as shown also in Figures 56 and 57.

Lightly cement the shank into position. Most shanks have one slightly curved end. Place the shank so the little curve extends into the sole. Use a shank that extends at least ¾ inch under the heel for a more stable feeling to your shoes (study Figure 57 for a guide).

Fig. 57.
Cement the shanks into position.

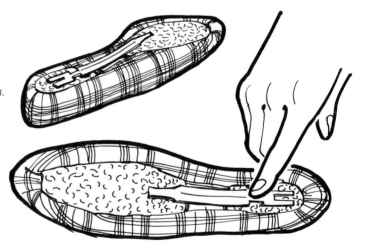

You now have the shoes ready for the soles and heels.

VIII
ASSEMBLING
THE SHOES

You have almost finished a pair of shoes!

See chapter X for a discussion on heels—how to choose the right heels for your shoes, and how to salvage them from old shoes.

1. Covering the Heels

Cut two sections of the fabric with a heel cover pattern made from your original heel, or wrap some material around the heel and make a pattern. You may cut the fabric on either the bias or the straight of the material, depending on the design of your fabric.

Cut the fabric generously at first. Apply a thin coat of cement over the entire back of the heel. Remove any lumps in your cement that would spoil the smooth effect of the heel covering. Wrap the material around the heel cementing in place as you proceed.

Check the heels for design placement of the fabric, as you can lift and replace at this point. Cut the material closer to the contour of the heel, leaving a "lapover" of about ¼ inch all the way around the heel (see Figures 58a, b, and c).

Fig. 58a.
Wrap fabric around the heel to make
the pattern.

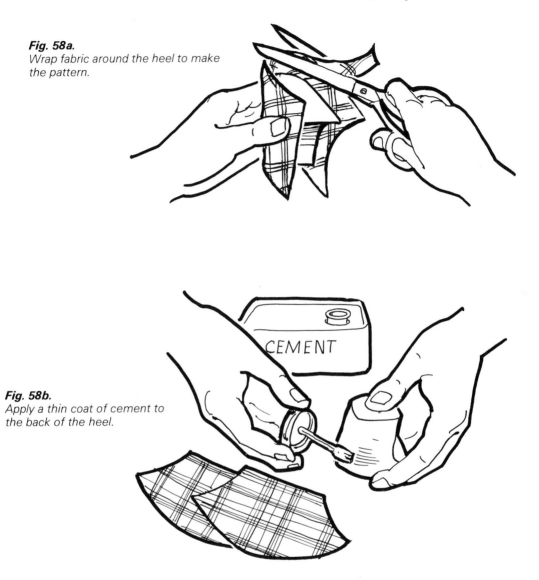

Fig. 58b.
Apply a thin coat of cement to
the back of the heel.

Fig. 58c.
Apply the fabric to the heel and
trim to ¼ inch all around the
heel.

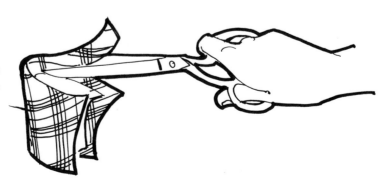

Notch the fabric around the top of the heel, and cut slashes in the curved areas so the material will easily fold over the edges as shown in Figure 59. Now apply a thin coat of cement to the areas of heel and fabric where the ¼ inch of material will fold over as illustrated in Figure 60. Set the heels aside for a few minutes. When the cement dries, stick all the edges down (see Figure 61).

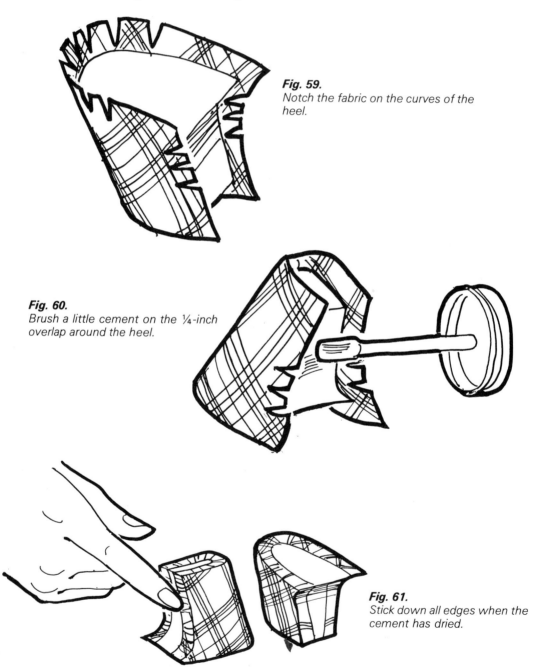

Fig. 59.
Notch the fabric on the curves of the heel.

Fig. 60.
Brush a little cement on the ¼-inch overlap around the heel.

Fig. 61.
Stick down all edges when the cement has dried.

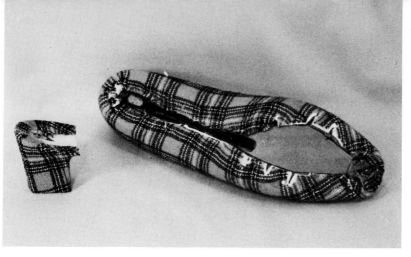

Heel and shoe are ready to be cemented together (see Figure 61).

2. Attaching the Heels to the Shoes

Hold the heel in the proper place on the shoe and make a white chalk line around the shape of the heel as in Figure 62. Choose chalk you can brush off when you finish.

Fig. 62.
Hold the heel up to the shoe and mark with chalk.

This cement holds stronger than nails if you apply it generously. Since the heels must set for at least a half hour after the cement is applied, make a little "holder" as I have done, to enable you to keep the heels steady while they are drying. I have used a piece of Styrofoam, but you could also use flower clay for a holder. The tops of the heels must lay flat so that the cement doesn't run off.

Fold a piece of corrugated cardboard into a triangle and tie or tape together to balance the shoes so that the cement doesn't run off onto the sides of the shoes.

Brush the cement over the entire top surface of the heels. Apply cement right to the edge. Now add about one teaspoon of cement to the center and put the heels in their holder and set aside (see Figure 63).

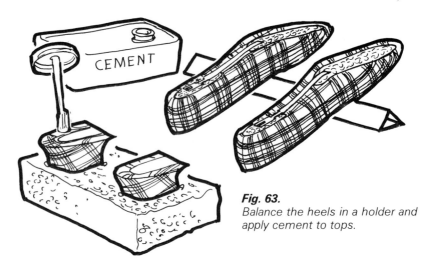

Fig. 63.
Balance the heels in a holder and apply cement to tops.

Apply a coating of cement to the area of the shoe inside the chalk line. If you miss a spot, the heel will not adhere in that place. Now add about one teaspoon of cement into the center, and balance the uppers on the triangle as shown in Figure 64. The shoe will readily absorb this cement so add another teaspoon in the same area, saturating the area with cement. Don't brush around the chalk line a second time; one application will work in that area. Sometimes the heel absorbs the cement so quickly you want to add a little more cement to the center of the heels also.

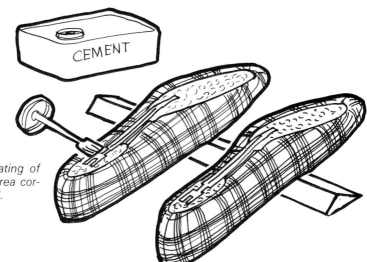

Fig. 64.
Apply a generous coating of cement to the shoe area corresponding to the heel.

Attaching the heels to the shoes (see Figures 64 and 65).

When all parts dry—at least around the outer edges of the cemented areas—you can attach the heels to the shoes. I like to wait until they have dried at least a half hour and sometimes longer.

Place the heels in the exact position on the shoe, as you *can't remove them* for a second try. If you find that the materials have left a little gap in some spots around the edge where the heel joins the shoe, you can run a needle under the fabric on the shoe and pull it down to the heel, as shown in Figure 65.

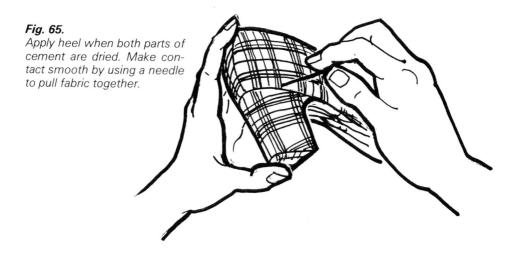

Fig. 65.
Apply heel when both parts of cement are dried. Make contact smooth by using a needle to pull fabric together.

Do not try on the shoes at this point. You may spoil the shape of the shoes before you attach the soles.

3. Cutting and Preparing the Soles

Even though you made a master pattern of the sole from the shoes that formed your lasts, measure it on your new shoes before cutting the leather. Pin a paper pattern of the sole to the bottom of your shoes. Make adjustments so that you have a perfect pattern. The shape of the sole will follow the contour of the pattern for your innersole, but will be a bit larger all the way around. In the heel area, or "breasting," the contour changes to correspond to the shape of the heel. The sole should match the outside edge of the shoe but not extend beyond the shoe. Until you become more experienced with the leather, I suggest that you cut this breasting area larger than the heel. You can trim to size after applying the sole to the shoe.

Trace the sole pattern on the right side—smooth side—of the leather using a ball-point pen. Turn your pattern over so that you will have both right and left soles as illustrated in Figure 66. Cut out the soles with your leather scissors. Hold the scissor blades straight so that you don't get a slant-edge cut. Be sure to cut exactly on the line (see Figure 67).

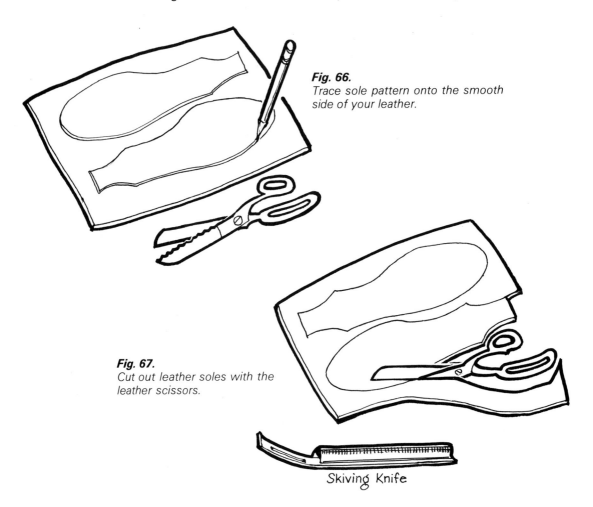

Fig. 66.
Trace sole pattern onto the smooth side of your leather.

Fig. 67.
Cut out leather soles with the leather scissors.

Skiving Knife

4. Using the Skiving Knife

Before you begin to "skive" on your leather, practice on a scrap. While not really difficult, you must practice. Skive off the area at the edges of the sole near the instep to make it appear thinner. Leave the *center* of the leather, which goes over the shank area, at its full thickness. Skive off the entire rough side of the leather at the place where the sole extends down inside the heel—the breasting. Make this paper thin (see Figure 68).

Fig. 68.
"Skive" off the leather in the areas indicated.

Skiving the leather on the sole (see Figure 68).

Smooth the edges of the leather with fine sandpaper. Color the edges with liquid shoe polish if you wish as shown in Figures 69a and b.

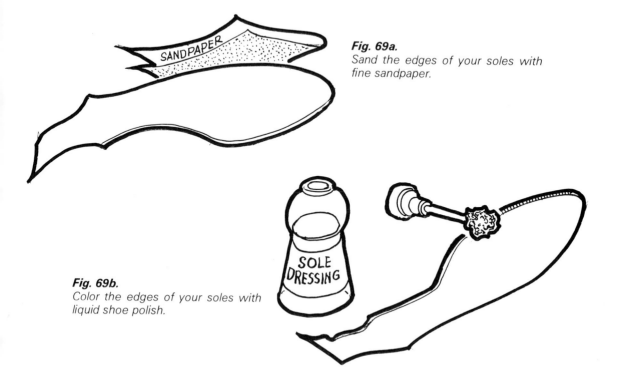

Fig. 69a.
Sand the edges of your soles with fine sandpaper.

Fig. 69b.
Color the edges of your soles with liquid shoe polish.

5. Attaching the Soles

Hold the soles up to the shoes and make a chalk line on the shoe in the area corresponding to the sole as shown in Figure 70.

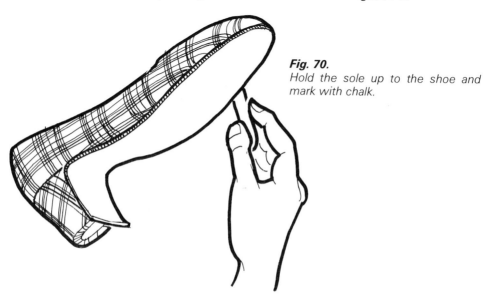

Fig. 70.
Hold the sole up to the shoe and mark with chalk.

Apply a thin coat of cement to the entire rough side of the leather sole. Sometimes a piece of leather appears quite smooth even on the "rough" side. In this case I "rough" up the area with a piece of metal sandpaper before applying the cement. Instead of the sandpaper, you can make a series of crosshatch cuts with a razor blade. This will enable the cement to grip the leather better (see Figure 71).

Fig. 71.
Apply cement to entire surface of the rough side of the sole.

Apply a coat of cement to the entire bottom of the shoes in the same corresponding area as the sole. Cover up to the edge next to the chalk line. The cardboard triangle will balance the shoes while the cement dries (see Figure 72).

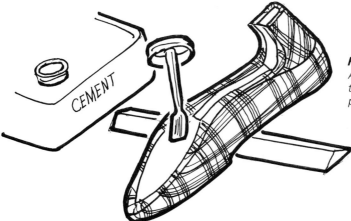

Fig. 72.
Apply cement to the entire bottom of the shoe in the corresponding area to the sole.

Let all sides of the cement dry completely. This will take at least a half hour and probably longer. Do not try to stick the soles to the shoes until both sides feel dry to the touch. Begin applying the sole at the toe of the shoe. Carefully place the sole so that it makes exact contact with the cemented areas of the shoes.

Since you can't pull up the sole and replace it, you must work carefully. Think "edges"—if you make contact on all the edges first, the center of the leather will stretch or ease into place (see Figures 73a and b).

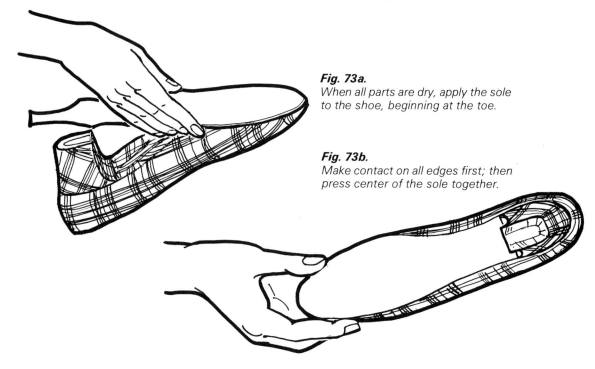

Fig. 73a.
When all parts are dry, apply the sole to the shoe, beginning at the toe.

Fig. 73b.
Make contact on all edges first; then press center of the sole together.

Press all the edges around the shoes; then put one hand inside the shoe and make contact all over the sole. Trim off the excess leather at the heel area with small curved scissors as shown in Figure 74. When you get more experienced, you can cut the breasting perfectly to size before cementing it into place.

Fig. 74.
Trim the "breasting" even with the heel.

6. Attaching Heel Lifts

When we wore thin heels, I went to the local shoe repairman to apply the lifts on the heels. With thicker heels and the area at the tip larger, you can easily *cement* a lift in place (follow the illustrations in Figures 75a, b, and c).

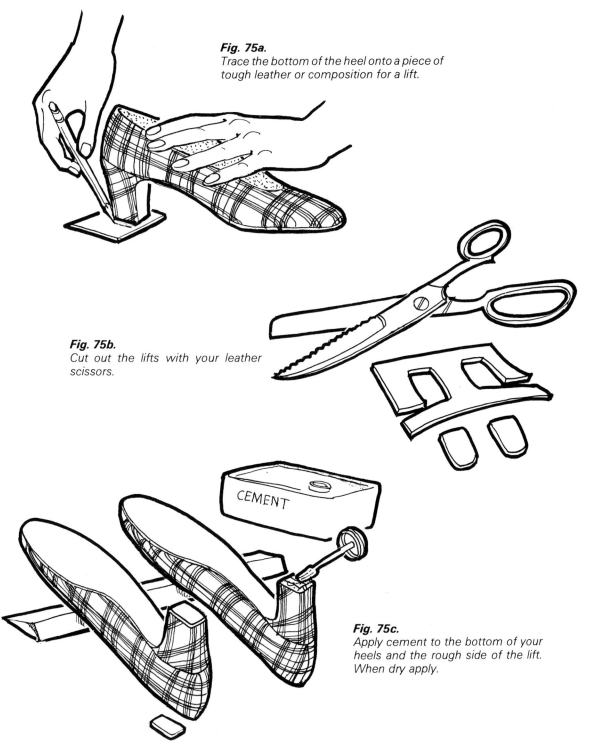

Fig. 75a.
Trace the bottom of the heel onto a piece of tough leather or composition for a lift.

Fig. 75b.
Cut out the lifts with your leather scissors.

Fig. 75c.
Apply cement to the bottom of your heels and the rough side of the lift. When dry apply.

Trace the bottom of your heel onto the tough leather or composition material for the lift. See chapter X about the type of leather to use for the heel lifts. Cut out the lift with your leather scissors. Sand the edges smooth. Apply black shoe polish to the edges of the heel lift. Rough up the area either with metal sandpaper or with the crosshatching technique used on the soles.

Apply cement to the rough side of the lifts, and the bottoms of your heels. Use your triangle to balance the shoes while the heel tips dry. When all parts are dry, join them together.

Now you can think of ways to decorate your shoes.

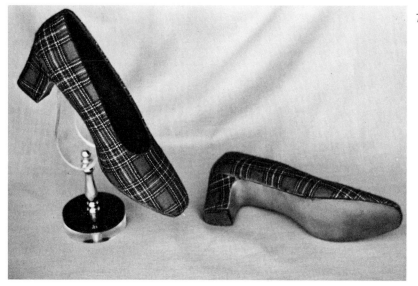

The finished shoes!

IX
THE
DECORATIVE
TOUCH

The *insole* adds a decorative touch as well as comfort to your shoes. Make it of felt, fabric, or leather. Use your pattern for the cardboard innersole as a guide to cut the *insole.* Cut the insole ⅛ inch larger except for the area inside the front of the shoe from the ball of the foot forward. See Figure 76 as a guide in cutting the insole shape.

If you wish to use felt, perhaps to match the lining of the shoes, chalk your pattern on the felt. Cut with pinking shears or plain scissors. Apply a little cement to the inside of the shoes and insert insole as shown in Figures 77a and b.

I like to make the decorative insole from fabric. Follow this easy method for a professional-looking insole.

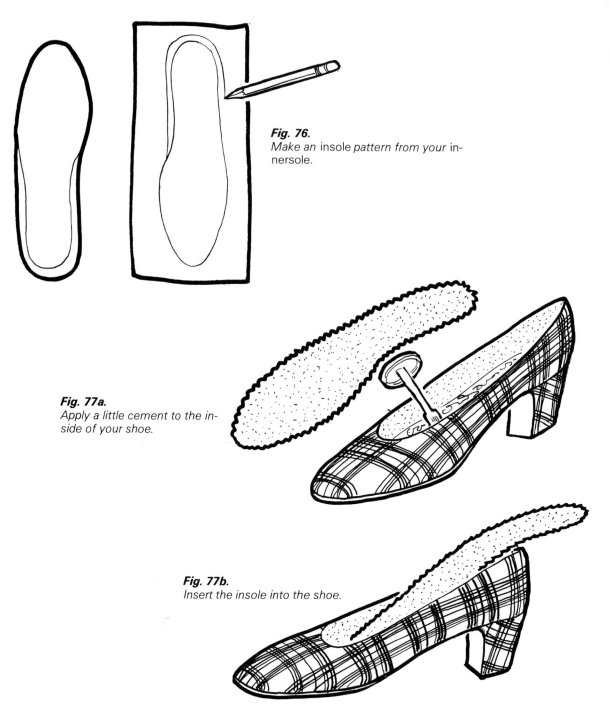

Fig. 76.
Make an insole *pattern from your in-nersole.*

Fig. 77a.
Apply a little cement to the in-side of your shoe.

Fig. 77b.
Insert the insole into the shoe.

1. Making a Fabric Insole

Follow the instructions shown in Figures 78a, b, c, and d.

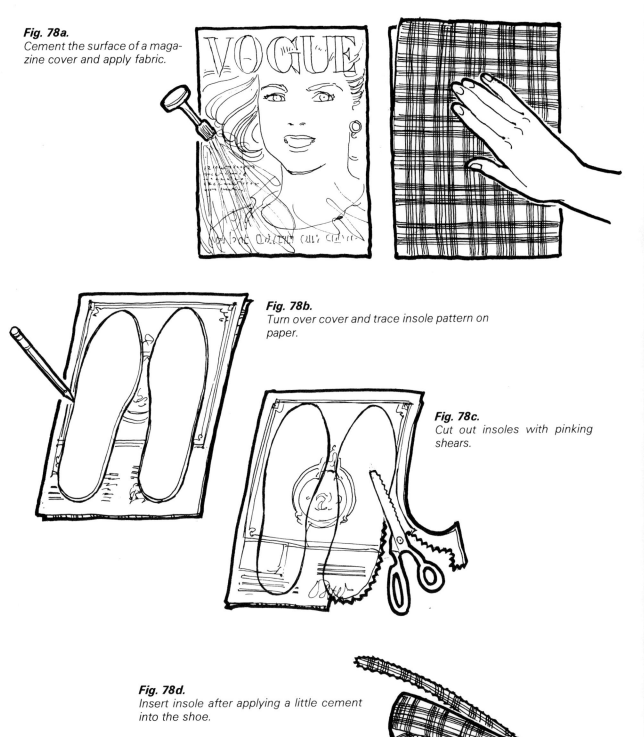

Fig. 78a.
Cement the surface of a magazine cover and apply fabric.

Fig. 78b.
Turn over cover and trace insole pattern on paper.

Fig. 78c.
Cut out insoles with pinking shears.

Fig. 78d.
Insert insole after applying a little cement into the shoe.

A cover from a magazine gives the stiffness for the insole. Apply a *thin* coating of cement or white glue over the entire surface of the cover. Press your fabric onto the cemented surface. Rub your fingers over and over so that each of the fibers adheres to the magazine cover.

When dry, turn your work over and trace out two copies of your insole pattern onto the paper, making sure to reverse one. Cut out with a pinking shears.

2. Applying the Insole

Apply cement or glue to the cardboard innersole inside the shoe. You need not cover the entire innersole with cement. Insert the insole into the shoe as shown in Figure 78d. Because you cut this pattern ⅛ inch larger than the cardboard innersole—from the ball of the foot back to the heel—you can place the insole so that it covers all the cardboard edges.

3. Making a Tailored Bow

Cut a piece of lightweight cardboard or buckram 1 inch by 5 inches long. If you select cardboard, check the direction of the grain. The 5 inch length should "roll." Apply a light application of glue or cement onto one side of the cardboard and apply the fabric. Trim, leaving approximately ⅓ inch on the sides to fold over. Apply glue to the ⅓ inch foldover area plus the cardboard. Stick the edges down. Bring the ends together by "rolling" the cardboard or buckram. Staple or sew the center together.

Cut a piece of bias fabric 2 by 2 inches. Fold edges and sew around the center of the bow. Secure a crushed look with your stitches. Follow the instructions in Figure 79.

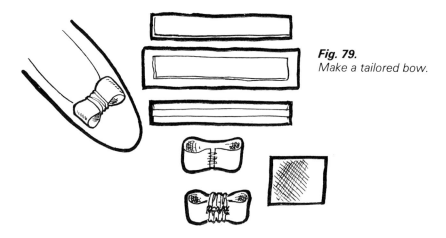

Fig. 79.
Make a tailored bow.

Before attaching the bows, hold them onto the shoes to decide the exact spot for placement. You can use bows to minimize the length of your shoes. When you determine the exact spot for placement make a chalk mark on the top of the shoe to guide you in cementing. Apply cement to the top of the shoe and to the back of the bow. When both sides are dry, apply the bow. Pinch tightly to the shoe so the bond will become secure.

I like to coordinate the bow with the covering on the heel using a lightweight suede leather, or a man-made suede. Sometimes you can find a perfect color of leather to accent a pattern in your fabric.

4. Making a Tie Bow

Cover a piece of heavy string with bias fabric. Each bow will use about 8 inches of string and bias fabric. Tie into a bow and tie the ends tightly. Cut close to the tied end (see Figure 80).

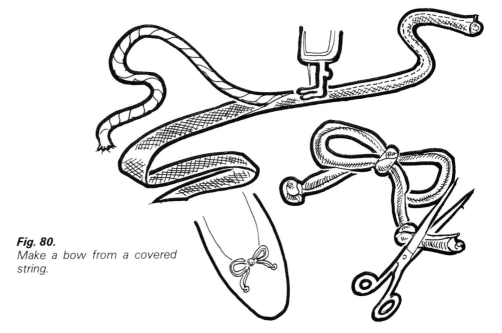

Fig. 80.
Make a bow from a covered string.

Cement or stitch the bow into place on top of the shoe.

Instead of using fabric and string for the tie you may find ready-made ribbon to match or accent your shoes as shown in Figure 81.

Fig. 81.
Trim the shoe with ribbon.

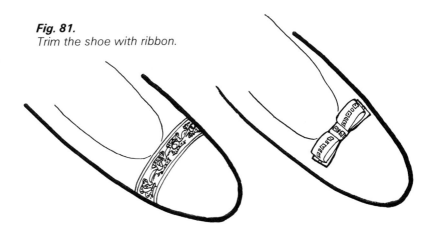

5. Butterfly Buckle

Cut a butterfly shape from your buckram scraps. Use the graph in Figure 82 for a guide. You will need at least three thicknesses of the buckram for each buckle. Wet the buckram with concentrated liquid laundry starch and let the three layers dry together over a rounded surface, such as a ball. When dry, glue fabric onto each butterfly buckle, and cement to the tops of your shoes (see Figure 83).

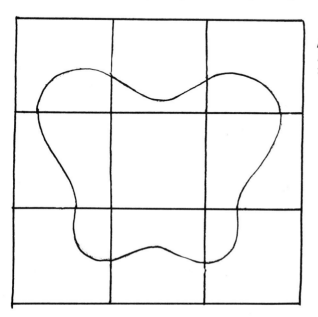

Fig. 82.
Each square represents one inch. Use this graph as a guide for butterfly bow.

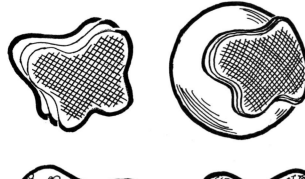
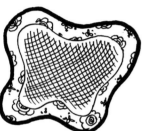
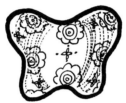

Fig. 83.
Make a butterfly bow from scraps of buckram.

6. Flat Buckle

Cut a piece of cardboard following Figure 84 as a guide. Pad the top with a piece of blanket padding or several thicknesses of felt. Cover with fabric or lightweight leather. Secure with glue or cement on the back. Cement onto the vamp of your shoes (follow illustrations in Figure 85).

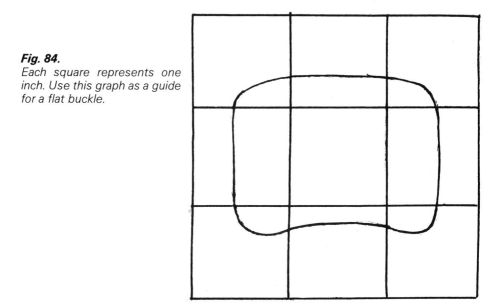

Fig. 84.
Each square represents one inch. Use this graph as a guide for a flat buckle.

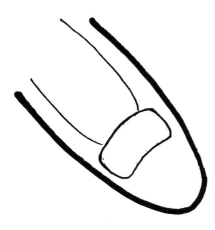

Fig. 85.
Make a flat bow from cardboard, padding, and leather.

7. Eyelet Tie

Attach eyelets or grommets into the sides of your shoes. Lace with ribbon and tie. You can get different effects with eyelets as shown in Figure 86.

Study the illustrations in Figures 87a and b and Figures 88a, b, and c for more ideas on trimming your shoes.

Fig. 86.
Attach eyelets or grommets for unusual lacing effects.

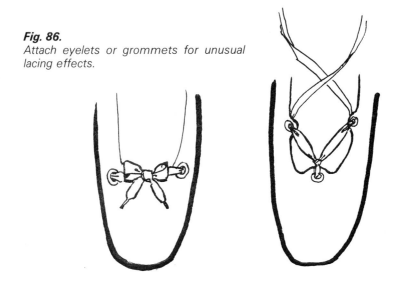

Embroidered toe and heel

Fig. 87a.
Hand embroider toe and heel of shoe.

Leather heel and toe

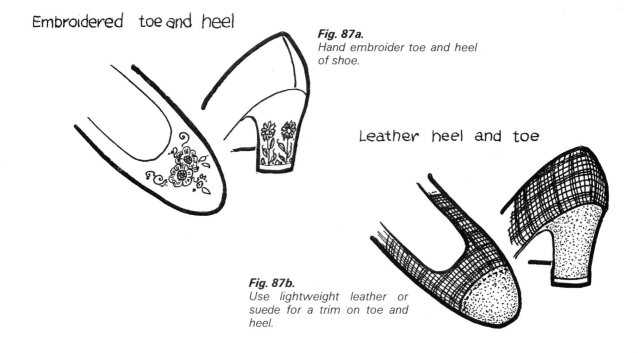

Fig. 87b.
Use lightweight leather or suede for a trim on toe and heel.

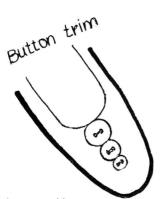

Button trim

Fig. 88a.
Trim with three pearl buttons.

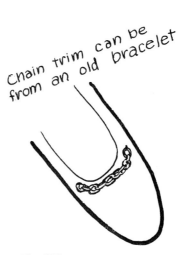

Chain trim can be from an old bracelet

Fig. 88b.
Use sections of chain from a discarded bracelet or necklace for trim.

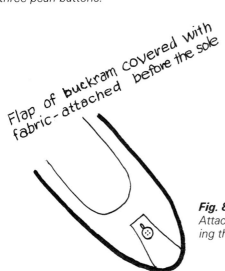

Flap of buckram covered with fabric-attached before the sole

Fig. 88c.
Attach flap with button before applying the soles.

Cotton floral low-heeled pumps.

Double knit fabric pumps with long skirt to match.

Gold silk print pumps with long skirt to match.

Silver brocade pumps with flat bow trim.

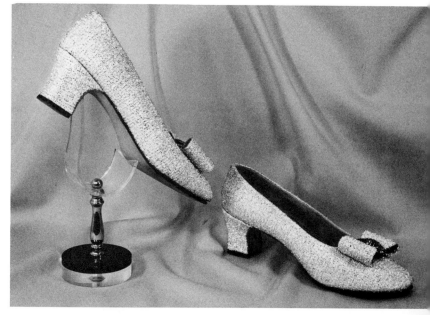

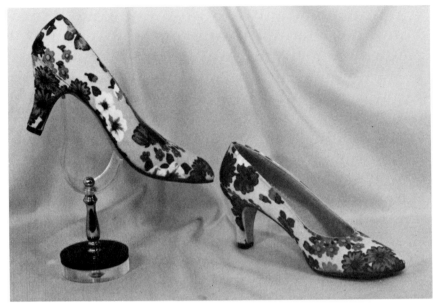

High heel linen print pumps.

Double knit pumps with street-length skirt to match.

X
MATERIALS
AND SUPPLES
FOR SHOEMAKING

Materials salvaged from old shoes reduces much of the cost of materials for making shoes. Perhaps you think a pair of worn shoes couldn't contain anything of value. But heels with the old coverings removed look like new, and buckles will easily polish for reuse.

RECLAIMED MATERIALS

1. Heels

The pair of shoes you dismantled for making your lasts provides you with a master pattern for heel size. This size offers a measurement for collecting heels from old shoes. With the coverings and heel lifts removed, they look as good as new. Your friends' old shoes or bargain shoes from a rummage sale can also provide you with heels if they are the proper height for your last. (See Figures 89a, b, and c for instructions on removing heels from old shoes.)

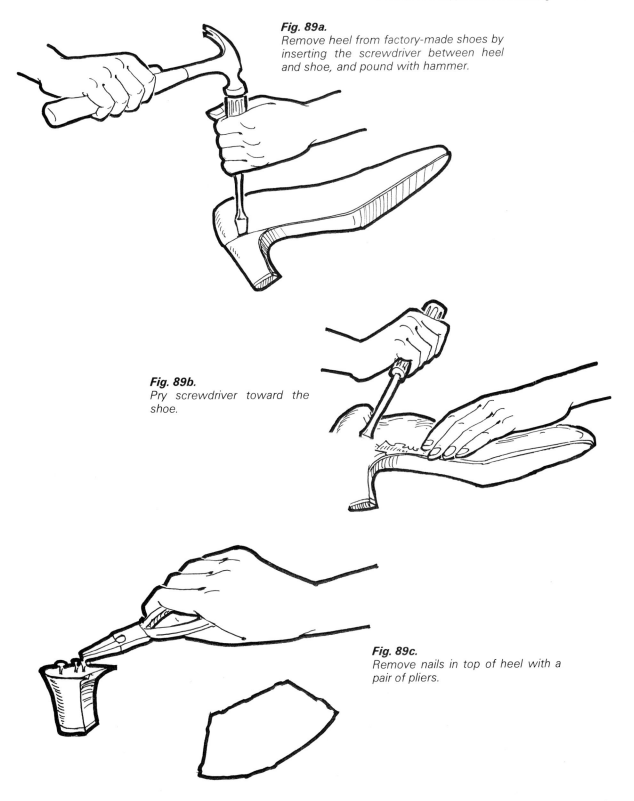

Fig. 89a.
Remove heel from factory-made shoes by inserting the screwdriver between heel and shoe, and pound with hammer.

Fig. 89b.
Pry screwdriver toward the shoe.

Fig. 89c.
Remove nails in top of heel with a pair of pliers.

Heels vary greatly, including height, angle or pitch, and thickness. These guides will aid you in choosing a proper heel: Figures 90a, b, c, d, and e.

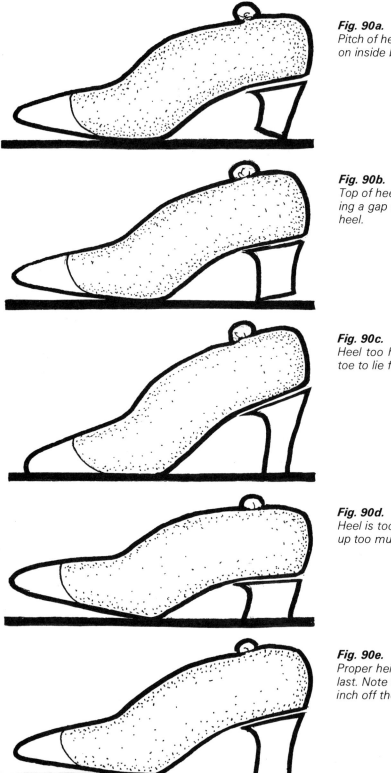

Fig. 90a.
Pitch of heel is too steep, causing a gap on inside bottom of heel.

Fig. 90b.
Top of heel is too flat for this last, causing a gap on the outside bottom of the heel.

Fig. 90c.
Heel too high for the last, causing the toe to lie flat on the floor.

Fig. 90d.
Heel is too low, causing the toe to turn up too much.

Fig. 90e.
Proper height and pitch of heel for this last. Note the toe of the last is about ½ inch off the floor.

All heels carry a large number on the top. This number indicates the circumference around the top of the heel. It does not refer to the height or style of the shoe but indicates the width of the shoe in the heel area. All heel manufacturers rely on these standard numbers. Each size differs only $1/16$ inch in width so several sizes may fit the same last if the height and pitch are correct.

If you don't have the right heels for a pair of shoes, you can cement a thickness of heavy cardboard or leather to the bottom of the heel to make it a bit higher. Or you can make heels lower by sanding or cutting off to the desired height. Your covering will hide this construction. You can also adjust the shape of your last under the heel area to fit the heel.

In chapter XII on sandals with heels I suggest using heels with covering all around. These heels are more suitable for sandals than pumps; however they can be used on either.

Your local shoe repairman may sell you heels, but old shoes offer the most economical source. Comparatively speaking, purchasing new heels can cost more than any other item in the shoes.

A screwdriver and hammer make removing the heels from factory-made shoes easy. Pry the screwdriver into the joining of the heel and the shoe and pound with the hammer. Turn the handle toward the shoe with the tip of the screwdriver into the heel. If you turn the screwdriver against the heel, you may damage the top. When the heel begins to loosen move the screwdriver to a new spot as described in the illustrations in Figures 89a, b, and c.

Reclaiming the heels from the shoes you make requires a different process. Since you attached the heels with shoemakers' cement, you must dissolve the cement to remove them. When I wish to reclaim materials from the shoes I have made, I pour about ¼ cup of cement thinner at the base of each counter of the shoe. I place the shoes in a can with an airtight lid and leave them sealed overnight. The parts separate easily.

2. Shanks

This metal brace reinforces all shoes at the arch. Collect shanks from old shoes. After removing the heels as described in Figures 89a, b, and c, the end of the shank becomes exposed. Pull the sole away with a pair of pliers and lift the shank out (see Figure 91).

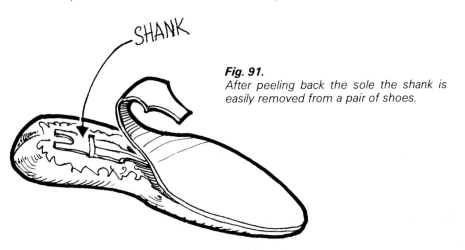

SHANK

Fig. 91.
After peeling back the sole the shank is easily removed from a pair of shoes.

Shanks vary in length and curve. You will want to use a shank that fits securely next to the curve of the arch on your last. A shank should extend under the heel at least ¾ inch. This adds necessary stability to your shoes. Even very low-heeled shoes need shanks.

If shanks curve too much to fit your arch, place them on a concrete or anvil surface and hit the high part of the curve with a hammer. Hold one end of the shank when you hit it, or the shank will fly across the room. Several blows will remove the curve. After each blow compare the curve of the shank for fit to the arch of the last. You cannot replace the curve once you remove it.

3. Cardboard

You will need good sturdy cardboard for an innersole in your shoes and to attach to the bottoms of your lasts. Artists' illustration board is best, but "gift" box type is also suitable.

4. Padding Inside the Shoes

Pieces of an old wool blanket or heavy wool fabric work best for padding because of the resiliency of wool. Some rubber rug padding is all right if it is not too thick, but foam rubber is too thin.

5. Trims

Save all buckles, bows, and trims from old shoes. Even though you don't plan to use them immediately, build a collection for inspiration in designing some new shoes. Renew any metal trims from old shoes by cleaning with a steel wool pad or some dry steel wool. Spray the metal with a clear acrylic spray or paint with clear nail polish. They will look like new!

PURCHASED MATERIALS   Look in your phone book for Leather Findings, Shoe Findings, Leather Goods, or Hobby Shops, or see Sources of Supply for some mail-order sources. If you live in a small town, ask your local shoe repairman where he buys his materials. Perhaps he will tell you when the salesman from a shoe findings company will call on him, and you can place an order.

1. Leather for the Soles

Use tooling leather, weight approximately $6/7$ ounce. Sometimes leather stores sell scraps of tooling leather. Form the habit of carrying a tracing of your sole pattern in your handbag. When you happen upon a source for this leather, you can check your pattern on scraps large enough to use. Of course, you can save money by purchasing a half of hide of leather.

You can use thinner leather for the soles, but first laminate two thicknesses of the leather together with shoemakers' cement. This dries to form a heavier piece of leather.

2. Cement

Barge Cement, a well-known brand, is a good shoemakers' cement; however, you will find others that work equally well.

When you purchase your cement, buy a can of cement thinner too. The cement will evaporate and needs to be thinned enough to penetrate the leather. Read the instructions on the container of cement. These cements consist of highly flammable chemicals, so do not inhale. I always work in a well-ventilated area when I use the cement.

3. Leather Scissors

Leather scissors make the job of cutting the soles very easy. With a smooth blade on the top and a serrated blade on the bottom, the scissors cut through any thickness of leather or heavy material but will not cut thin or lightweight fabrics. In addition to leather shops, or shoe findings companies, you can order leather scissors from your hardware store.

4. Skiving Knife

Skiving makes the leather thinner. An injector razor blade inserted in this knife "pares" away at the leather and reduces the thickness from the rough side. The leather part of the sole that extends down the inside of the heel, known as the "breasting," needs thinning to eliminate bulk. With practice you can learn to control the thickness you remove. Change the blades of your skiving knife with a pair of long-nose pliers. Never try to insert a new blade with your fingers as you can easily cut them.

5. Counters

The counters provide the stiffness in the back of the heel. While the market offers many types of counters, I prefer a ladies' fiber composition counter. You may also find them referred to as "fiberboard" counters. Sometimes the supplier labels them "R" and "L." Unless the counter extends down under the arch on the inside of the shoe, "R" and "L" counters differ so slightly you can use them interchangeably.

The counter also determines the height of your shoe at the back of the heel. If you wish to make the back of the heel area higher or lower, trim the counter—not your upper pattern.

Sometimes you can salvage counters from factory-made shoes. To salvage them you must remove dozens of little nails in the bottoms of the counters and this often damages them. I recommend purchasing new counters.

6. Composition or Heavy Leather for Heel Lifts

Heel lifts require a tougher grain of leather than the soles. They take more direct wear. You can purchase a small piece of this leather or a man-made composition material from a shoe findings company. Some shoe repairmen will sell you a piece of this leather or composition material, but mostly they would prefer attaching the lifts for you.

7. Stapler

A heavy duty stapler is used in making sandals. I use the Ace Clipper Model No. 702. It is available at stationery and office supply stores. See Sources of Supply for a mail-order source.

8. Adhesive Tape or Continuous Filament Tape

Used for reinforcing the straps on sandals. I buy the wide roll and tear strips the width I want to use. Filament tape can be purchased in stationery or variety stores.

9. Fabric Glue

You will need some kind of fabric glue when making sandals. See Sources of Supply, in case you don't find it in your local fabric store.

MISCELLANEOUS ITEMS

1. Buckram

Buckram, a heavy even fiber material saturated with sticky starch or sizing, shapes the shoes. When wet it becomes very pliable, and when dry it becomes stiff again. This quality allows the shoe to take on the shape of the last when dried. Purchase buckram in fabric or upholstery shops. See Sources of Supply for a mail-order source.

2. Muslin

Muslin forms an interlining when combined with the buckram inside the shoes. You can substitute a lightweight cotton fabric for the muslin. I have used pieces of old sheets, but I caution you not to use fabric so worn it may tear when you put the uppers onto the lasts. Any fabric store sells muslin.

3. Felt for Lining Shoes

Felt makes a good lining for your shoes because it shrinks and dries smoothly against the last. I have used all types of felt: wool, cotton, and wool/rayon combinations. They all work well. Any fabric store sells felt.

You can use a lightweight leather for the lining; it will wear longer but cost more.

4. Laundry Starch

Buy a concentrated liquid laundry starch at the grocery store. A tablespoon of this concentrated starch will make the toe of the shoe stiffer.

5. Plaster of Paris

Purchase plaster of Paris at a hardware store, paint store, building supply house, or a hobby shop. I suggest that you do not store your plaster of Paris on a cement floor. The moisture from the cement will deteriorate the plaster. Keep it in a warm, dry place.

6. Large Eye Needle, Thimble, and Nylon Yarn

Use these to hand sew the upper to the last. I find nylon the strongest "thread" for hand sewing. Since you must pull your stitches tightly, you cannot sew with yarn or thread that breaks easily. Choose any color.

XI
CHOOSING THE OUTER FABRICS FOR YOUR SHOES

Almost any fabric will form the outer part of the shoe. The inner construction remains the same for all types. The buckram inside the shoe shapes and strengthens the uppers. For the upper, I prefer to work with wool, cotton, or linen in a medium-weight fabric. These assure you of good results, especially for a beginner.

1. Fabrics

Avoid bulky or lumpy fabrics. Loose weave fabrics cause some trouble in the seam edges. An iron-on stayflex provides a backing on brocades or loose weave materials.

Iron all materials flat to straighten the grain of the fabric. You need not prewash or shrink fabric for the outer part of your shoes. If it shrinks, all the better—the upper only fits more smoothly onto the last.

When you choose a plaid, striped, or checked fabric, you must match your uppers exactly in design. While some plaids or stripes look lopsided in design, occasionally you can reverse the fabric to get a uniform look to the shoes. For floral prints I often make the shoes out of two different sections of the fabric so they purposely do not match.

Anytime you cut out a dress or garment and you plan to match shoes, add your basic pattern for the upper and heel covering to your dress patterns so you save enough material in the proper design. An extra ⅛ yard will assure you enough fabric for shoes.

I keep a special box of fabrics to make an additional pair of shoes to match an outfit. Sometimes a dress or skirt will become a favorite of mine and I wear it so much I want to make a new pair of shoes to match.

Sometimes you may choose organdy, voile, or lace for a special pair of shoes. I helped a bride-to-be make her wedding dress with shoes to match. For these fragile fabrics baste a thin lining of the same color to the back of the fabric with small uniform stitches. Leave these stitches in the fabric until you wet the upper to form it onto the last; then you can pull them out. Iron-on staflex offers another way to give body to thin materials. Test a piece of fabric with the staflex backing first because it may change the appearance of the fabric color.

2. Man-made Suedes and Suede Cloth

I have experimented with man-made suedes and suede cloths in recent years. Suede *cloth* costs less, sews easily, and looks as good as suede. Suede *cloth* has a fabric-bonded back. The *man-made suedes* resemble suede leather on both sides. You can sew and form these suedes and suede cloths into beautiful shoes!

Use a needle size 14 or 16 with approximately 10 stitches to the inch when sewing on suede or suede cloth. Tiny stitches cut through the suede. Practice on a small scrap to determine the proper tension and length of stitch.

If the suede cloth or man-made suede does not travel freely under the pressure foot, put a piece of wax paper under the material. Then it will move freely. Tear off the paper from the back when you finish sewing the seam.

Suedes and suede cloths have a nap so check its direction before cutting. You can feel the nap with your fingers.

3. Leather

After you complete a few pairs of shoes and thoroughly test your pattern, you will want to make a pair of leather shoes. Purchase leather in a department store or upholstery shop. See Sources of Supply for a list of leather suppliers. Tandy Leather Company sells a booklet providing professional information about sewing on leather. It also includes information on how to order leather, types of leather, and other pertinent facts.

Use a leather needle size 14 or 16 to sew on leather and 8 to 10 stitches per inch. I urge you to buy leather needles for your sewing machine even though regular needles will sometimes work on leather. You get best results with a leather needle. Keep your leather needles in a special box so you don't use them on other fabrics by mistake. They look so much like regular sewing machine needles; I inspected them under a magnifying glass to see the difference. The leather needle has a knifelike point whereas the regular needle has a tapered point. If you use them on fabric the knifelike point may cut the threads of your fabric.

When sewing on leather you must remember you cannot rip your stitches as they will leave a hole.

WATERPROOFING YOUR FABRICS   Some of the fabrics will need waterproofing. I waterproof fabrics that soil easily, such as silks, brocades, or any other *light-colored* materials. Velvets require waterproofing in spite of dark color.

1. Silicone Waterproofing

You can buy various brands of silicone waterproofing, liquid or spray. They primarily protect furniture, raincoats, boots, and shoes from moisture and dirt. Check with your grocery store, department store, or shoe repair shop for silicone waterproofing.

If you choose the liquid, put it into a shallow pan so that you can capture the leftover waterproofing to pour back into the bottle. Immerse only enough fabric to make the outer part of the shoes and a covering for the heels. After thoroughly saturating your fabric, hang it to dry in a well-ventilated area or out-of-doors. Whichever place you choose, put some papers under the line to catch the drips. You can also lay the fabric flat on a smooth *clean* surface to dry. If you have one little spot of grease or dirt on that area, you can ruin your waterproofing job!

Spray in a well-ventilated area and hang the fabric up to dry. Silicone waterproofing will leave an odor on the fabric, but it will disappear in a few days.

2. Waterproofing with Wax Paper

Wax paper will quickly waterproof the surface of cottons or linens. If you want to try it on other fabrics, experiment with a small scrap of the fabric.

Tear off two pieces of wax paper—each piece as large as the fabric. Lay one piece of the wax paper on the ironing board. Place the fabric between the two sheets of wax paper. Iron directly on the paper until the fabric absorbs the wax.

This method of waterproofing works well for fabrics used in making handbags. It gives the fabric body and a bit of stiffness that is desirable for handbags.

Black velveteen sandals with heels.

Multicolor silk pumps. Butterfly buckle trim. Handbag made from snap frame bag instructions.

Assortment of shoes.

Assortment of handbags.

Lavender plaid pumps with leather trim on toe and heel.

Multicolor rayon print pumps, bag, and blouse.

Silver brocade pumps with evening bag.

Mary with shoes.

Silver brocade with combination bow and antique steel cut buckle trim.

Beige suede-cloth low-heeled pumps with skirt.

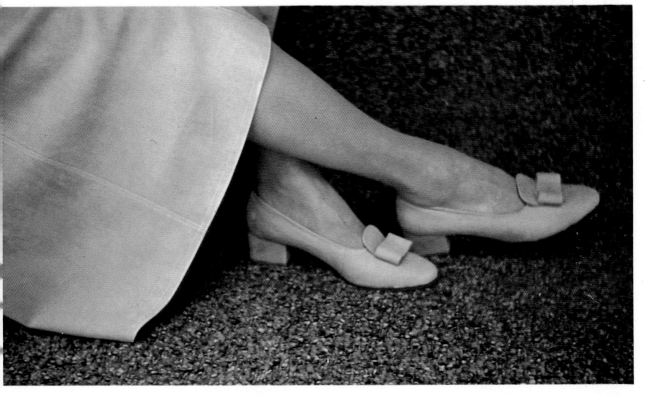

Red brocade pumps with small evening bag made from coin purse snap frame. Rhinestone button trim on bag.

Snakeskin print vinyl fabric pumps with snap frame bag.

Orange floral linen pumps with snap frame bag. Moss green velvet trim.

XII
MAKING SANDALS
WITH HEELS

Sandal making offers unlimited creativity. They are fun to make and require very little material. You need only purchase leather for the soles and shoemakers' cement; the other items you can salvage from old shoes, *as suggested in chapter X.*

MATERIALS NEEDED
Heels probably salvaged from an old pair of shoes. Choose a heel 1 to 1½ inches high, the type you cover on all sides. These heels are very suitable for sandals and require a different process than the pumps for making and attaching the soles. After learning this method you can interchange it with your pumps if you wish.

Shanks salvaged from an old pair of shoes.

Cardboard. Artist's illustration board works well, or use some other firm heavy cardboard.

Lightweight wrapping paper for your pattern.

Fabric glue.

Adhesive, cloth, or continuous filament tape, for strengthening the straps.

2 buckles. These you can salvage from old shoes.

Leather for soles and heel lifts.

Heavy duty stapler.

Sandals need more width than closed pumps. The foot spreads without the restriction of a pump. Make a barefoot sandal even wider than one worn with stockings. The outline of the foot changes shape when it rests on a heel. To establish your sandal shape follow this method:

1. Making a Foot Pattern

Using a piece of cardboard for your pattern, "roll" it in the arch section, and place the cardboard onto the heel. Place your foot on the cardboard and trace the outline as shown in Figure 92. Unless your feet are different sizes, you need do this only once. Reverse the pattern for the other foot. Using this outline of your foot, smooth the lines. Trace the top of the heel shape on the back of your pattern so the contour of the sandal will follow the shape of the heel (see Figure 93).

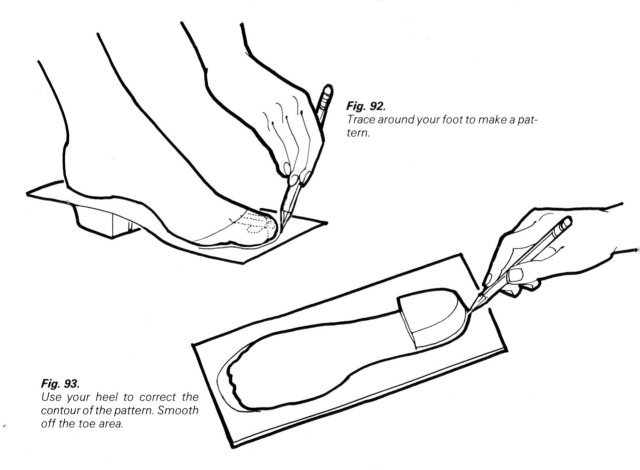

Fig. 92.
Trace around your foot to make a pattern.

Fig. 93.
Use your heel to correct the contour of the pattern. Smooth off the toe area.

2. Making the Innersoles

Cut four of these foot shapes in a firm cardboard. Remember cardboard has a grain, and you will want the arch sections to "roll" with the grain.

Make a definite bend in the platform base at the ball of the foot. This will indicate the placement of the shank.

Cut bias strips of fabric about 1½ inches wide, long enough to cover the edges of all four of the cardboard innersoles. Stretch the bias fabric around the edge of each innersole and secure with a stapler as shown in Figure 94. If you stretch the bias, it will contour flat around the curves. At the joining, overlap fabric and staple firmly. I like to place the joining either at the instep or under a strap.

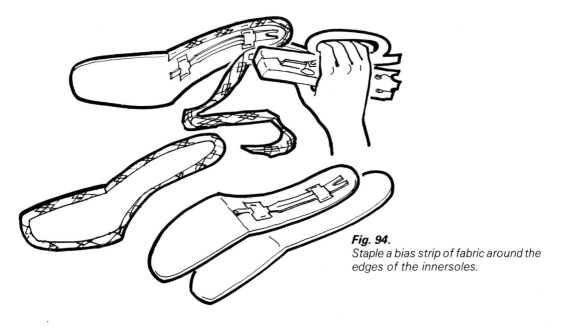

Fig. 94.
Staple a bias strip of fabric around the edges of the innersoles.

Two of these innersoles you will attach to the soles and heels and the other two to the uppers. Sandwiched together they make a pair of sandals! Begin by making the *bottom* of the sandals: a combination of the sole, heel, shank, and bottom innersole.

Attach the shanks to the bottoms of the innersoles with tape or staple a strip of fabric over the shanks. Choose shanks that will extend at least one inch under the heel. The strength of the arch depends on a good portion of the shank cemented to the top of the heel (see Figure 95).

Fig. 95.
Secure the shanks in place with strips of fabric or adhesive.

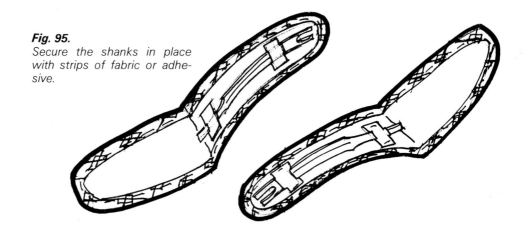

3. Covering the Heels

Heels that are covered all around have a little "trough" under the arch to hide the edges of the fabric. Apply a thin coat of cement all around the heel, making sure to cement into the trough. Wrap the fabric around the heel, smoothing into place. Trim the fabric leaving ⅛ inch on each side to force tightly into the trough using a knife or large needle.

Trim the fabric to ¼ inch all around the top and the bottom of the heel. Cut notches to remove excess fabric. Apply a light coat of cement onto the heel and the fabric edge. When cement dries, press all edges down firmly. Follow the instructions in Figures 96a, b, c, d, and e.

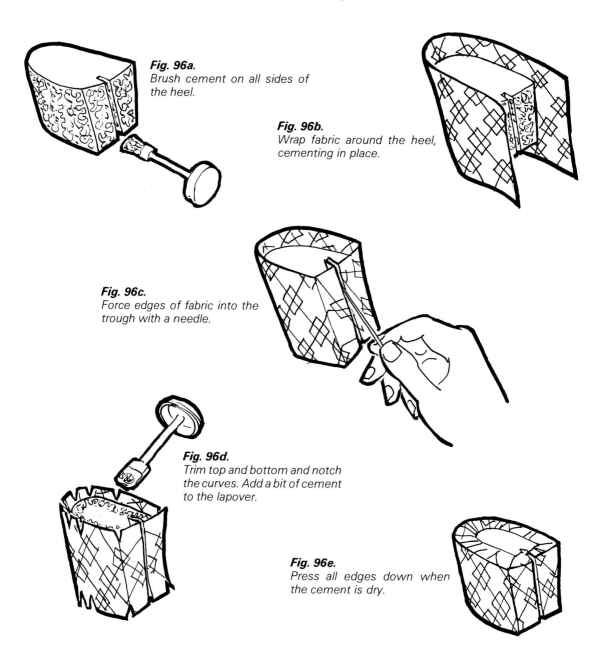

Fig. 96a.
Brush cement on all sides of the heel.

Fig. 96b.
Wrap fabric around the heel, cementing in place.

Fig. 96c.
Force edges of fabric into the trough with a needle.

Fig. 96d.
Trim top and bottom and notch the curves. Add a bit of cement to the lapover.

Fig. 96e.
Press all edges down when the cement is dry.

4. Making a Sole Pattern

Your sole pattern will duplicate the same contour as the innersole, except it stops where it meets the heel and extends under the heel with a small tongue.

Make your sole pattern by placing the heel onto a tracing of the innersole. Mark across the straight side of the heel. Draw a small tongue on the end of your pattern. Make sure the sole pattern measures exactly the same width as the heel where they join (see Figure 97).

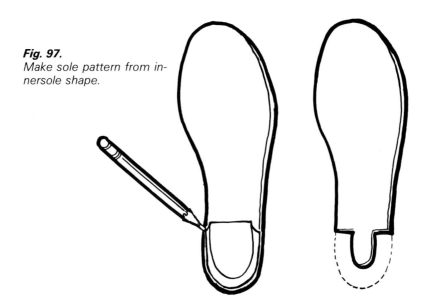

Fig. 97.
Make sole pattern from innersole shape.

5. Cutting the Soles

Trace your sole pattern onto the smooth side of the leather with a ball-point pen with a fine clean line. *Reverse* the pattern for the second sole! Cut on the pen line with your leather scissors.

Skive off a thin strip of leather on the *rough* side of each arch section of the soles (review chapter VIII). Skive the *smooth* side of the leather on the tongue. Smooth the edges of the soles with fine sandpaper and color with black liquid shoe polish if desired. Follow the instructions in Figures 98 and 99.

Fig. 98.
Cut soles from leather.

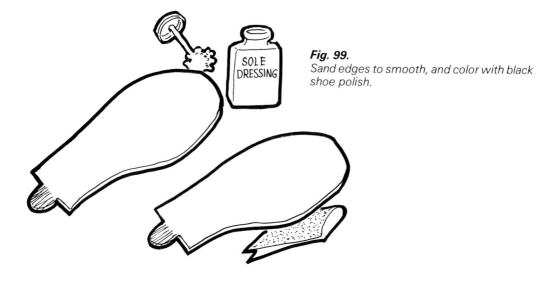

Fig. 99.
Sand edges to smooth, and color with black shoe polish.

6. Cementing the Soles

In order to get a good bond, rough up the leather before applying the cement. A metal scraper or sandpaper does a good job. Or you can use the crosshatching method with a razor blade (see Figure 100). Slant the blade so you don't cut through the leather. Your cardboard innersole needs roughing up so the cement will penetrate. Repeat the crosshatch method.

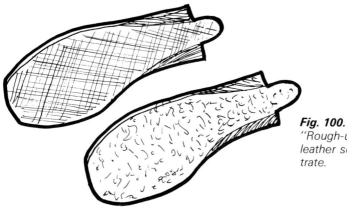

Fig. 100.
"Rough-up" or crosshatch the leather so the cement will penetrate.

Apply cement to sole and the corresponding area on the innersole. Set aside to dry before sticking together. Sometimes the cement gets ready to stick together in about 15 minutes, but this does depend on the thinness of your cement, the porousness of the leather, and the climate.

Beginning at the toe, press the leather soles to the innersoles (see Figure 101).

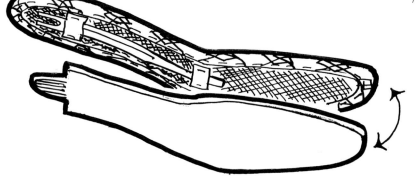

Fig. 101.
After applying cement to innersole and sole press two parts together.

7. Attaching the Heels

See chapter VIII for directions to attach heels. Definitely use a generous amount of cement to firmly secure the top of the heel to the end of the shank.

MAKING THE UPPER PART OF THE SANDAL

1. Making Your Upper Pattern

The graph in Figure 102 shows a pattern size 7½A. To make your size trace the pattern onto a graph enlarging the squares to 1 inch each. Since each full shoe size varies approximately 3/16 inch, cut the pattern and enlarge or decrease as indicated in Figures 103a, b, and c.

Fig. 102.
Pattern graph for upper. Make each square 1 inch.

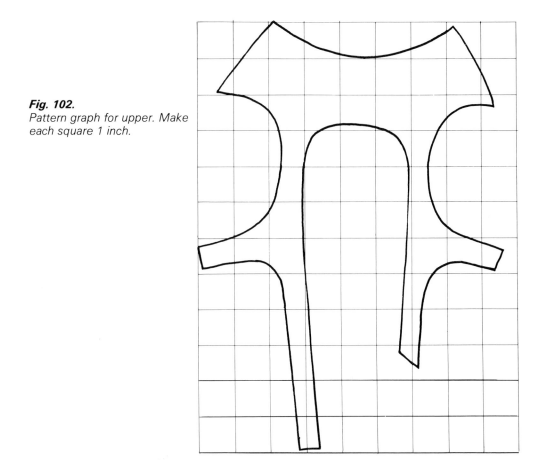

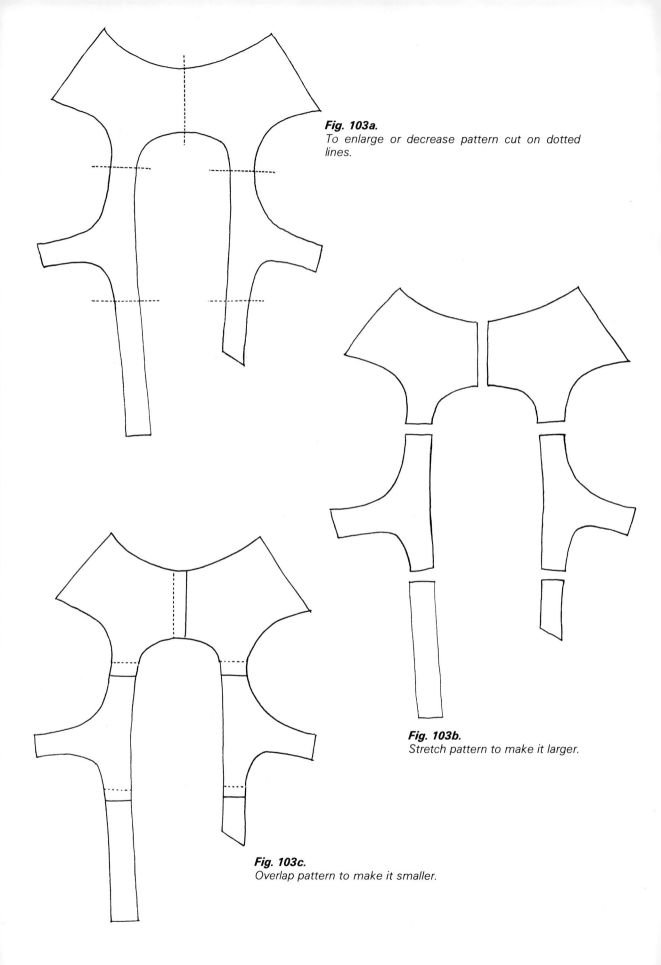

Fig. 103a.
To enlarge or decrease pattern cut on dotted lines.

Fig. 103b.
Stretch pattern to make it larger.

Fig. 103c.
Overlap pattern to make it smaller.

2. Making the Upper for Your Sandals

Trace two patterns from lightweight wrapping paper. Cut them out very accurately. Glue these paper patterns to the *wrong* side of the fabric using a fabric glue (see Figure 104).

Fig. 104.
Glue pattern to the wrong side of your fabric.

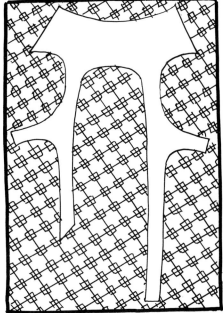

Cut away the fabric, leaving ¼ inch all around the edges of the paper. Apply fabric glue to these edges and fold back as illustrated in Figure 105. Dry and press either by ironing or place between the pages of a magazine overnight. If you use the magazine method, place a piece of white paper on top of your fabric so the magazine doesn't leave a stain.

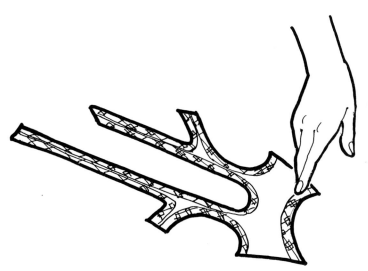

Fig. 105.
Trim and glue the edges down onto the wrong side of the pattern.

Apply strips of adhesive, fabric, or continuous filament tape to the back of the straps for strength as shown in Figure 106.

Fig. 106.
Reinforce the straps with strips of tape.

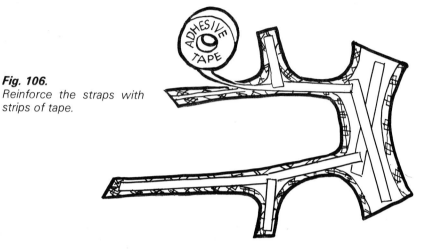

Topstitch the upper onto a piece of lightweight leather or felt for a lining. Cut away lining around the edge, and attach the buckles on the end of the longer strap (see Figure 107).

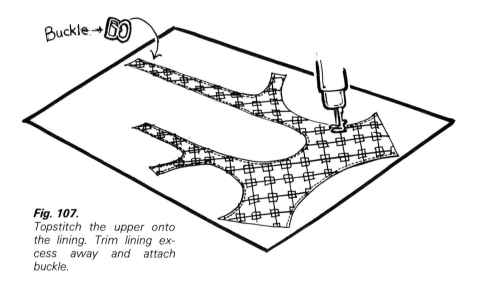

Fig. 107.
Topstitch the upper onto the lining. Trim lining excess away and attach buckle.

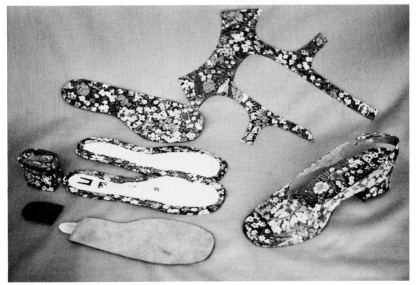

Sandals with heels; one as-sembled and one in parts (see chapter XII).

3. Assembling the Sandals

Place your foot onto the platform base and determine the placement of the straps by holding the upper part of the sandal onto your foot as shown in Figure 108. Staple the straps into place.

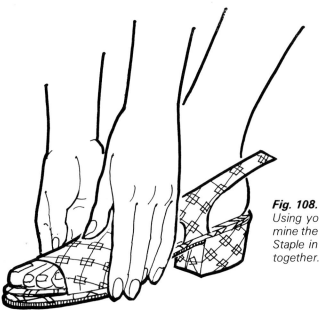

Fig. 108.
Using your foot for a last, deter-mine the placement of the straps. Staple in place and cement shoe together.

Before cementing the two innersoles together, rough up the cardboard innersoles using a razor blade or sharp knife to make cross-hatch marks through the surface of the cardboard so that the cement will penetrate. Apply a generous coating of cement to all four sides.

When the cement dries to the touch, you can stick the parts together. Begin at the toe area and carefully press the two sections together.

4. Making an Insole

Using your sole pattern, trace two insoles on thin cardboard or a heavy magazine cover. Cut out, at the same time trimming away about ⅛ inch all around the edge. Apply a thin coat of cement to one side of each of the insoles. Press down firmly onto the reverse side of your fabric. Cut away fabric, leaving ¼ inch to fold over the edges. Apply a light brushing of cement to the edges and fold over. Cement the insole into the sandals. Follow the instructions in Figures 109a, b, and c.

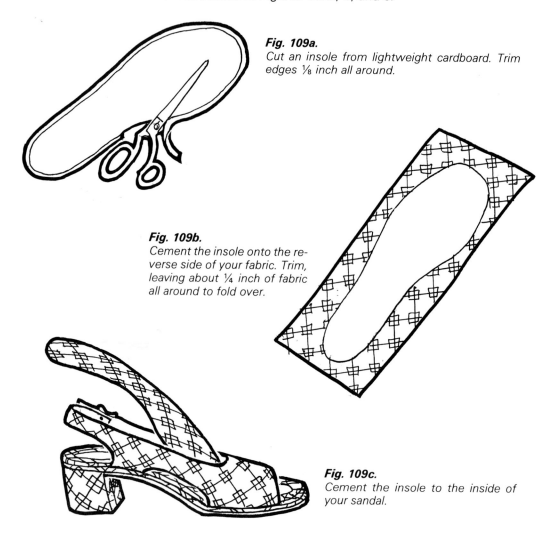

Fig. 109a.
Cut an insole from lightweight cardboard. Trim edges ⅛ inch all around.

Fig. 109b.
Cement the insole onto the reverse side of your fabric. Trim, leaving about ¼ inch of fabric all around to fold over.

Fig. 109c.
Cement the insole to the inside of your sandal.

5. Attaching a Lift to Your Heels

Chapter VIII gives directions for applying heel lifts.
    Your sandals will become more wearable if you make a matching handbag.

XIII
MAKING
HANDBAGS

A handbag to match your shoes seems a natural way to coordinate your outfit. I have chosen two simple styles to demonstrate. Either style easily adapts to any fabric or size.

Let's begin with the easiest one. This one piece, envelope bag you can make in an hour. I made this bag in the small flower print fabric to match the sandals with heels. To photograph it more clearly I made it again—just another hour's work—in a moss green vinyl material.

ENVELOPE BAG

1. Making Your Pattern

Using the graph in Figure 110 as a guide, make each square 1 inch. This will make a bag approximately 5 by 10 inches. If you wish to make your pattern smaller or larger, change the size of the squares on the graph. Cut your pattern from heavy paper or cardboard.

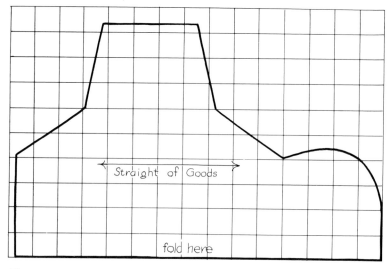

Straight of Goods

fold here

Fig. 110.
Pattern graph for envelope bag. Make each square 1 inch.

2. Materials Needed

Approximately ⅛ yard fabric or suede. This amount will vary depending on the size of your bag. Place your pattern on the straight of the goods.
    Staflex if fabric lightweight
    Felt for lining
    Large snap or button for closure

3. Sewing the Handbag

Trace your pattern onto wrong side of fabric with a fine clean ball-point pen or sharp piece of chalk. Cut at least ⅓ inch outside your pattern line. If you use staflex, iron it onto the wrong side of the fabric first, then trace pattern onto staflex.

    Place right side of fabric onto right side of lining. Sew on the pattern line, leaving an opening approximately 3 inches at front edge of bag as indicated in Figure 111. Trim seam allowance to ¼ inch all around. Clip corners and remove excess material on the curved edges by notching as shown in Figure 112.

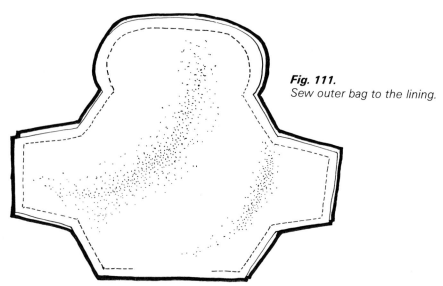

Fig. 111.
Sew outer bag to the lining.

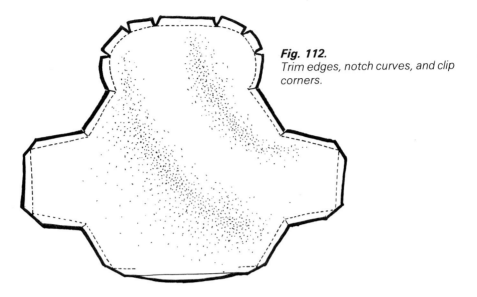

Fig. 112.
Trim edges, notch curves, and clip corners.

Turn right side out through the opening. Close the opening with hand stitching. Press flat. Pull out the corners with a needle or awl.

Topstitch all around the bag on the right side as illustrated in Figure 113. Even topstitching shows the difference between a professional- or amateurish-looking job, so take your time. I prefer a buttonhole twist for this topstitching and a rather large stitch. Practice on a scrap until you get the desired look. When I want to sew a very perfect topstitching, I hold my hand on the wheel of the sewing machine ready to control every stitch.

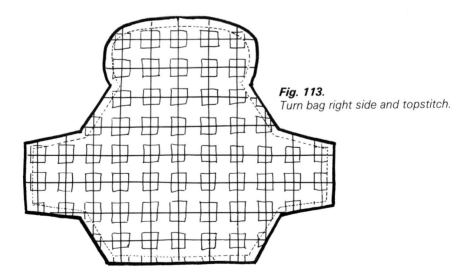

Fig. 113.
Turn bag right side and topstitch.

One piece envelope bag topstitched, as shown in Figure 113.

Sew the side seams of the bag by hand stitching the lining together. Use a double thread in your needle and carefully place each stitch so it does not show on the outside of the bag (see Figure 114).

Fig. 114.
Hand stitch corners together from the inside.

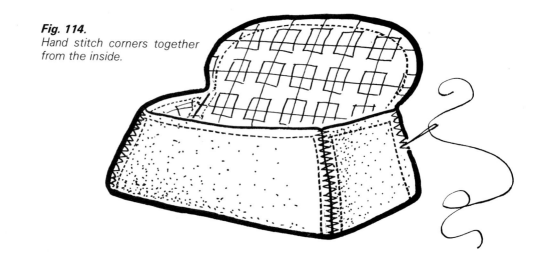

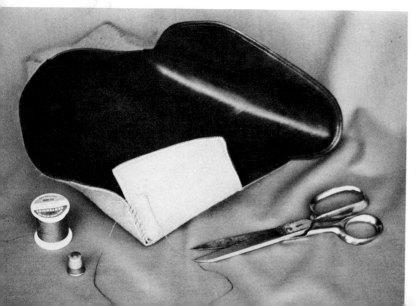

Sewing the side seams of the envelope bag (see Figure 114).

Sew a large snap or velcro for closing as shown in Figure 115. Add a buckle or button for trim if you wish. For an evening bag a fancy earring or clip makes a perfect trim. Remove the ear clip from the back with a pair of pliers and sew onto the flap.

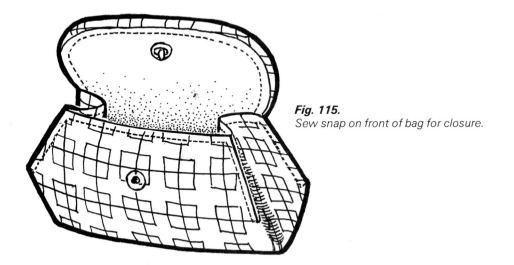

Fig. 115.
Sew snap on front of bag for closure.

The finished one piece envelope bag.

SNAP FRAME BAG   I always hesitated to throw away a handbag with a perfectly good snap frame and perhaps some nice brass trim. So I learned a simple way to make a new bag and insert it into the old frame. Before long I owned a drawerful of bags to match my shoes. My friends all offered me their worn handbags, and my large collection includes all sizes and shapes of frames.

The old handbag, ripped apart and flattened, makes your pattern for the new bag. This offers a good way to trace a pattern for an intricate cut, such as a bag with a gusset. But you needn't make the same shape or style. I like to experiment with a new pattern on the old frame.

1. Materials Needed

Old handbag with snap frame
Pliers
Screwdriver
White all-purpose glue
Large needle or awl
Fabric for the new bag (practically any kind if not too thick and
    heavy)
Iron-on staflex or iron-on pellon
Lining for the new bag (felt, silk, vinyl, faille, or lightweight leather)
Masking tape or adhesive tape
Compass or pencil with string

2. Removing the Old Bag from the Frame

If you want to use a frame in good condition on your new handbag without covering with fabric, protect the frame with masking tape before you begin to remove the old handbag. Leave the tape on the frame until you have finished your new handbag to protect it from scratches.

Begin at the hinge of the frame and grasp the fabric or leather close to the frame with a pair of pliers. Twist to pull the old bag out of the frame. Take a new grip every inch and continue across the frame until you remove the entire old bag (see Figure 116).

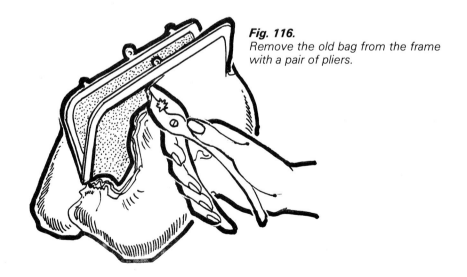

Fig. 116.
Remove the old bag from the frame with a pair of pliers.

After removing the old bag, open the channel of the frame slightly. Place a screwdriver into the channel and twist gently to open. Continue all the way around the frame, as shown in Figure 117.

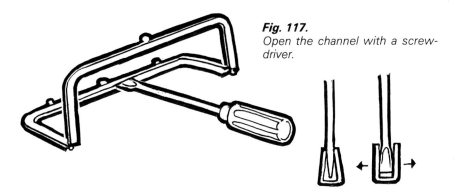

Fig. 117.
Open the channel with a screwdriver.

3. Making a Pattern for Your Bag

If you make a pattern from the pieces of your old bag, add seam allowance by opening all seams and pressing them flat before tracing the pattern. Don't use an iron on a leather bag. Wet the pieces thoroughly and flatten them out to dry.

You can create a new shape with the frame and a compass. Follow the diagrams in Figures 118 and 119.

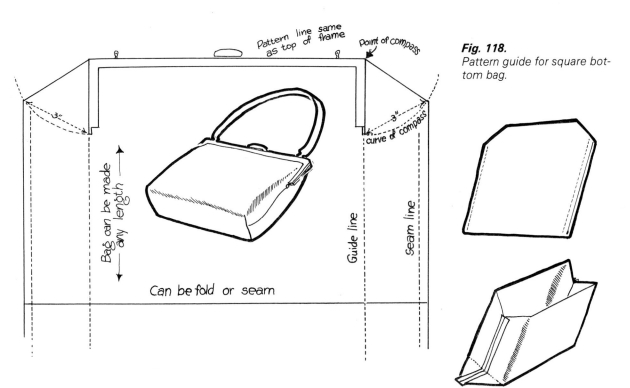

Fig. 118.
Pattern guide for square bottom bag.

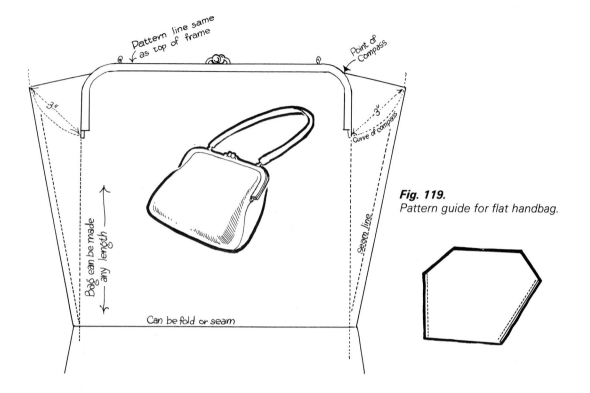

Fig. 119.
Pattern guide for flat handbag.

4. Cutting and Sewing Your New Bag

Cut your pattern from iron-on pellon or staflex. Iron onto the back of your fabric. Cut out around edge of the pellon or staflex as shown in Figure 120.

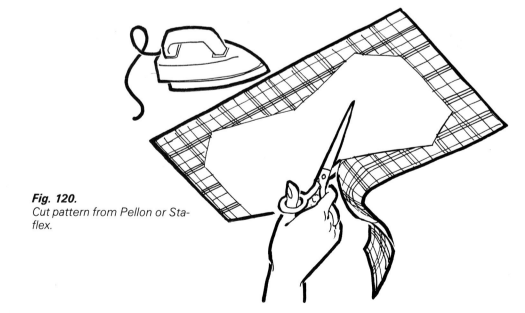

Fig. 120.
Cut pattern from Pellon or Sta-flex.

Sew small seams on each side of your bag. I find it a good idea to sew two rows of stitching very close together and trim away to a seam allowance of ⅛ inch (see Figure 121).

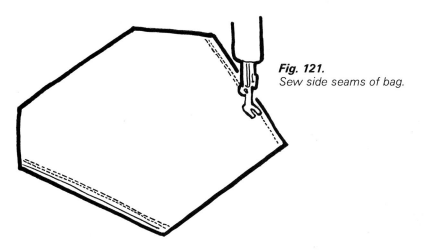

Fig. 121.
Sew side seams of bag.

Cut the lining from the same pattern, but make it ¼ inch smaller on each side. If you want a pocket on the inside of your lining, sew it on before you stitch the side seams of the lining.

Turn the outer section of the bag right side out and press. Leave lining with wrong side out and press.

You can give an added professional touch to your bag by stiffening the sides. Cut medium-weight cardboard ¼ inch smaller than the lining and pad the sides of the cardboard with foam rubber or felt as shown in Figure 122.

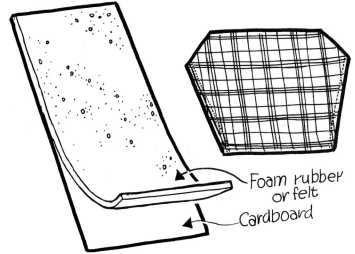

Fig. 122.
Pad the inside of the bag with foam or felt and cardboard.

Foam rubber or felt

Cardboard

Insert this padding between outer bag and lining (see Figure 123). Slip the lining into the outer bag and overcast the raw edges of the tops together as shown in Figure 124. If you own a zigzag machine, you can do this on the sewing machine with a large size stitch.

Fig. 123.
Insert padding between the bag and the lining.

Fig. 124.
Sew the tops of the bag and the lining together.

5. Covering the Frame with Fabric

Cut two pieces of bias fabric, wide enough to fit over the frame and leave almost ⅓ inch on each side to fold up into the channel of the frame. Apply a thin coat of white glue onto all parts of the frame, including the channel.

Stick the fabric onto the frame, making small slits to fit over loops or clasp. Fold the fabric up into the channel and push against the sides with an awl or large needle (see Figures 125, 126, and 127).

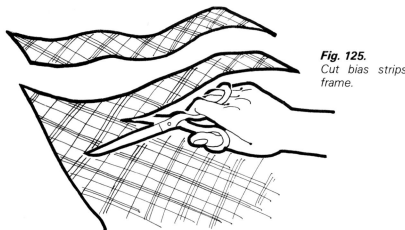

Fig. 125.
Cut bias strips for covering the frame.

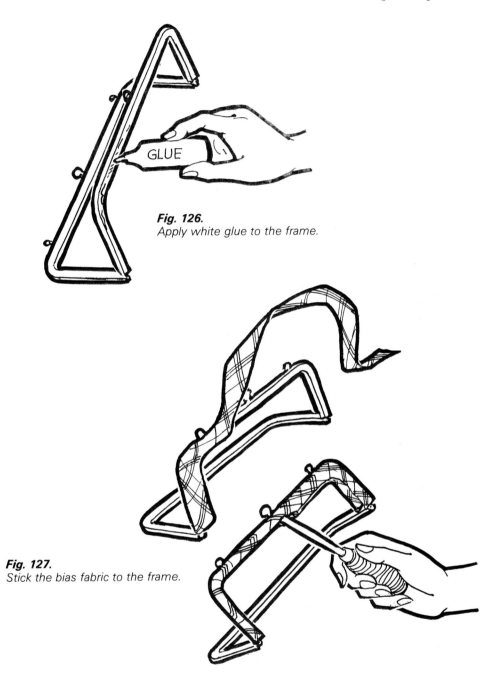

Fig. 126.
Apply white glue to the frame.

Fig. 127.
Stick the bias fabric to the frame.

6. Putting the Bag into the Frame

Insert white glue into the channel of one side of the frame (see Figure 128).

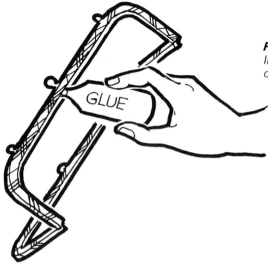

Fig. 128.
Insert white glue to the inside of the channel on the frame.

Beginning at the hinge, push the bag into the channel with a large needle or an awl, as illustrated in Figure 129. When you have completed one side put aside to dry before doing the other side.

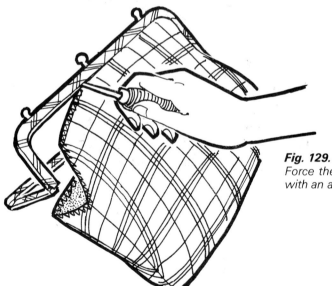

Fig. 129.
Force the handbag into the channel with an awl or needle.

When both sides feel dry, gently squeeze the frame together again by putting a table knife (or bread and butter knife) on each side of the frame, and squeeze against the knives with the pliers as shown in Figure 130. If you don't use the knives, you will bend or scratch the frame. Avoid use of good silver as the pliers will scratch the knives.

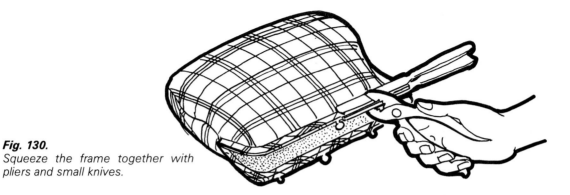

Fig. 130.
Squeeze the frame together with pliers and small knives.

7. Making a Handle for the Bag

Sometimes you need not change the old handle if it seems suitable in color and style to the new bag. This doesn't happen often, so refer to the illustrations in Figures 131a, b, c, d, and e for some suggestions for making new handles.

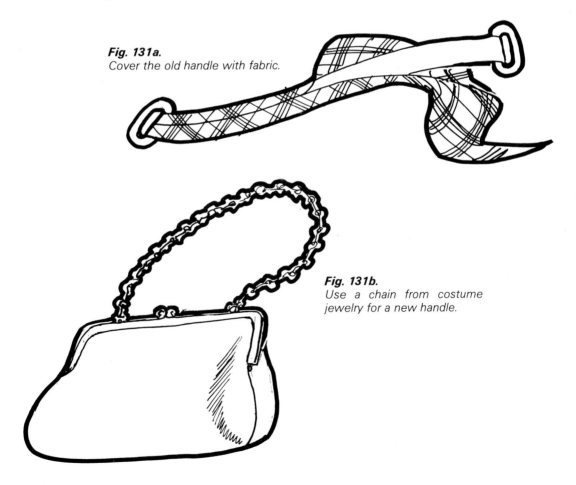

Fig. 131a.
Cover the old handle with fabric.

Fig. 131b.
Use a chain from costume jewelry for a new handle.

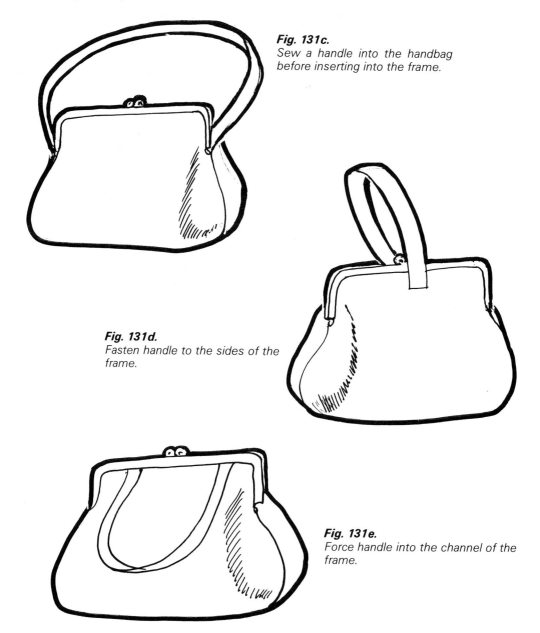

Fig. 131c.
Sew a handle into the handbag before inserting into the frame.

Fig. 131d.
Fasten handle to the sides of the frame.

Fig. 131e.
Force handle into the channel of the frame.

Now that you have made a handbag to match your shoes I suggest you begin another pair of shoes as soon as possible. Confidence comes with experience and soon you will find it is just as much fun to make your own shoes as it is to wear them.

When you have discovered the economy and enjoyment of the perfect fit with individual styling, you may never want to *buy* another pair of shoes.

Multicolor linen pumps and snap frame bag.

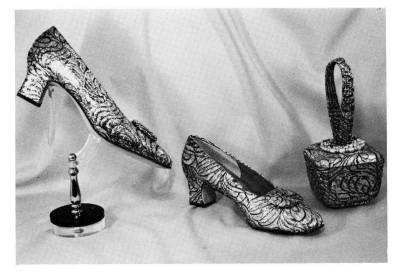

Brocade pumps with flat buckle trim. Evening bag to match made from plastic refrigerator container.

Snakeskin print vinyl pumps with snap frame handbag.

Gold brocade pumps with evening bag.

Red brocade pumps with small snap frame evening bag.

Gray suede-cloth pumps with antique buckle. One piece envelope bag to match.

SOURCES
OF SUPPLY

Look in the Yellow Pages of your telephone book under Shoe Findings, Leather Goods, or Leather Findings. If you live in a small community go to your local telephone office. They will have the phone books of nearby larger cities and you can obtain addresses from these directories.

Or you can talk to a local shoe repairman. He has to order his materials from a shoe findings company and perhaps you can get the name of the company from him, or he may order for you.

Here are the names of some companies you can write to for supplies:

Berman Leather Company
147 South Street
Boston, Massachusetts 02111

Colo-Craft
1310 South Broadway
Denver, Colorado 80210

Leathercrafters
25 Great Jones (E. 3rd) Street
New York, New York 10012

Amber Leather Company
2850 South Harbor Boulevard
Santa Ana, California 92704
(No Mail Order)
Tel.: (203) 627—9141
      (714) 754—0200

Ben Adams & Sons, Inc.
4933 Telegraph Avenue
Oakland, California 94609
or
819 North Wilson Way
Stockton, California 95205

J. P. Fliegel Co.
P.O. Box 505
Gloversville, New York 12078

The Leather Works
628 Emerson
Palo Alto, California 94301
Tel.: (415) 328—9602

C. S. Osborne & Co.
Harrison, New Jersey 07029
(Tools only)

Tandy Leather Company
3 Tandy Center
P.O. Box 2686
Fort Worth, Texas 76101
(Stores throughout the country)

The Chandlers Fabric Store
66 East Fourth Avenue
San Mateo, California 94401
Tel.: (415) 344—4516
(Source of buckram)

Baste 'N' Sew Gluestik
(fabric glue also used for holding
   ultrasuede or leather before
   stitching)

Available at:

Sewing Corner
150—11 14th Avenue
P.O. Box 420
Whitestone, N.Y. 11357

   or

Nasco
Fort Atkinson, Wisconsin 53538

INDEX